CogLab
on a CD

Experiments Prepared by
Greg Francis and Ian Neath
Purdue University

Instructional Material by
Angie MacKewn
University of New Brunswick

Danalee Goldthwaite
University of British Columbia

THOMSON

WADSWORTH

Australia • Canada • Mexico • Singapore • Spain • United Kingdom • United States

Publisher: Vicki Knight
Acquisitions Editor: Marianne Taflinger
Assistant Editor: Jennifer Wilkinson
Editorial Assistant: Nicole Root
Technology Project Manager: Darin Derstine
Marketing Manager: Lori Grebe
Marketing Assistant: Laurel Anderson

Advertising Project Manager: Brian Chaffee
Production Project Manager: Candace Chen
Print/Media Buyer: Rebecca Cross
Permissions Editor: Sommy Ko
Cover Designer: Natalie Hill
Printer: Webcom Limited

Printed in Canada
    5 6 7 07 06

ISBN 0-534-64067-2

For more information about our products,
contact us at:
Thomson Learning Academic Resource Center
1-800-423-0563
For permission to use material from this text,
contact us by:
Phone: 1-800-730-2214
Fax: 1-800-730-2215
Web: http://www.thomsonrights.com

Wadsworth/Thomson Learning
10 Davis Drive
Belmont, CA 94002-3098
USA

Thomson Learning
5 Shenton Way #01-01
UIC Building
Singapore 068808

Australia/New Zealand
Thomson Learning
102 Dodds Street
Southbank, Victoria 3006
Australia

Canada
Nelson
1120 Birchmount Road
Toronto, Ontario M1K 5G4
Canada

Europe/Middle East/Africa
Thomson Learning
High Holborn House
50/51 Bedford Row
London WC1R 4LR
United Kingdom

Latin America
Thomson Learning
Seneca, 53
Colonia Polanco
11560 Mexico D.F.
Mexico

Spain/Portugal
Paraninfo
Calle/Magallanes, 25
28015 Madrid, Spain

CogLab

on a CD

CONTENTS

Introduction to CogLab   i
Getting Started with CogLab   ii
Running a CogLab Experiment   iv
CogLab FAQ   ix

EXPERIMENTS

ATTENTION

Attentional Blink   2-3
   References
   Basic Questions
   Advanced Questions
   Discussion Questions
Simon Effect   4-6
   References
   Basic Questions
   Advanced Questions
   Discussion Questions
Spatial Cueing   7-9
   References
   Basic Questions
   Advanced Questions
   Discussion Questions
Stroop Effect   10-11
   References
   Basic Questions
   Advanced Questions
   Discussion Questions

PERCEPTION

Apparent Motion   12-13
   References
   Basic Questions
   Advanced Questions
   Discussion Questions
Muller-Lyer Illusion   14-15
   References
   Basic Questions
   Advanced Questions
   Discussion Questions

Signal Detection   16-18
    References
    Basic Questions
    Advanced Questions
    Discussion Questions
Visual Search   19-20
    References
    Basic Questions
    Advanced Questions
    Discussion Questions

NEUROCOGNITION

Brain Asymmetry   21-23
    References
    Basic Questions
    Advanced Questions
    Discussion Questions
Mapping the Blind Spot   24-25
    References
    Basic Questions
    Advanced Questions
    Discussion Questions
Receptive Fields   26-28
    References
    Basic Questions
    Discussion Questions

SENSORY MEMORY

Metacontrast Masking   29-30
    References
    Basic Questions
    Advanced Questions
    Discussion Questions
Modality Effect   31-32
    References
    Basic Questions
    Advanced Questions
    Discussion Questions
Partial Report   33-34
    References
    Basic Questions
    Advanced Questions
    Discussion Questions

Suffix Effect   35-36
   References
   Basic Questions
   Advanced Questions
   Discussion Questions

SHORT-TERM MEMORY

Brown-Peterson   37-38
   References
   Basic Questions
   Advanced Questions
   Discussion Questions
Irrelevant Speech Effect   39-40
   References
   Basic Questions
   Advanced Questions
   Discussion Questions
Memory Span   41-42
   References
   Basic Questions
   Advanced Questions
   Discussion Questions
Position Error   43-44
   References
   Basic Questions
   Advanced Questions
   Discussion Questions
Operation Span   45-46
   References
   Basic Questions
   Advanced Questions
   Discussion Questions
Sternberg Search   47-49
   References
   Basic Questions
   Advanced Questions
   Discussion Questions

MEMORY PROCESSES

Encoding Specificity   50-51
   References
   Basic Questions
   Advanced Questions
   Discussion Questions

False Memory   52-53
    References
    Basic Questions
    Advanced Questions
    Discussion Questions
Forgot It All Along   54-56
    References
    Basic Questions
    Advanced Questions
    Discussion Questions
Remember/Know   57-59
    References
    Basic Questions
    Advanced Questions
    Discussion Questions
Serial Position   60-61
    References
    Basic Questions
    Advanced Questions
    Discussion Questions
Von Restorff Effect   62-63
    References
    Basic Questions
    Advanced Questions
    Discussion Questions

SPEECH & LANGUAGE

Categorical Perception – Identification   64-66
    References
    Basic Questions
    Advanced Questions
    Discussion Questions
Categorical Perception – Discrimination   67-69
    References
    Basic Questions
    Advanced Questions
    Discussion Questions
Lexical Decision   70-72
    References
    Basic Questions
    Advanced Questions
    Discussion Questions

Word Superiority   73-74
 References
 Basic Questions
 Advanced Questions
 Discussion Questions

CONCEPTS

Absolute Identification   75-77
 References
 Basic Questions
 Advanced Questions
 Discussion Questions
Implicit Learning   78-80
 References
 Basic Questions
 Advanced Questions
 Discussion Questions
Mental Rotation   81-82
 References
 Basic Questions
 Advanced Questions
 Discussion Questions
Prototypes   83-84
 References
 Basic Questions
 Advanced Questions
 Discussion Questions

JUDGMENT

Monty Hall   85-86
 References
 Basic Questions
 Advanced Questions
 Discussion Questions
Risky Decisions   87-89
 References
 Basic Questions
 Advanced Questions
 Discussion Questions
Typical Reasoning   90-92
 References
 Basic Questions
 Advanced Questions
 Discussion Questions

Wason Selection Task   93-95
   References
   Basic Questions
   Advanced Questions
   Discussion Questions

Glossary   96-99

Introduction to CogLab

Welcome to the Cognitive Psychology Laboratory (CogLab™), a set of demonstrations of classic and current experiments and concepts from cognitive psychology. CogLab allows students to experience a variety of important experimental studies, which will help them understand the design of the study, the data, and the significance of the research.

CogLab On A CD will work on any operating system that adequately supports the Java programming language. This includes Microsoft Windows 98-XP and MacOS 8.5-X. Other operating systems may also work.

CogLab Demonstrations include:

Attention
Attentional Blink
Simon Effect
Spatial Cueing
Stroop Effect

Perception
Apparent Motion
Muller Lyer Illusion
Signal Detection
Visual Search

Neurocognition
Brain Asymmetry
Mapping the Blind Spot
Receptive Fields

Sensory Memory
Metacontrast Masking
Modality Effect
Partial Report
Suffix Effect

Short-Term Memory
Brown-Peterson
Irrelevant Speech
Memory Span
Operation Span
Position Error
Sternberg Search

Memory Processes
Encoding Specificity
False Memory
Forgot It All Along
Remember/Know
Serial Position
Von Restorff Effect

Speech & Language
Categorical Perception –
   Identification
Categorical Perception –
   Discrimination
Lexical Decision
Word Superiority

Concepts
Absolute Identification
Implicit Learning
Mental Rotation
Prototypes

Judgment
Monty Hall
Risky Decisions
Typical Reasoning
Wason Selection

Getting Started with CogLab on a CD

CogLab is a program that allows you to explore aspects of Cognitive Psychology by participating in various experiments. This version of CogLab is run off a CD. Start by inserting the CogLab CD into the CD drive of your computer. To start the CogLab program follow the instructions for your operating system, as discussed below.

Microsoft Windows 98-XP

The CogLab program should start automatically. You will know the program is loading if you see the following:

Depending on the speed of your computer, it may take a few minutes for the program to load. If you don't see the picture shown above, you may need to start CogLab manually. Use the file explorer to look at the files on the CD. Double click on the file called *COGLAB1.exe*.

MacOS X

Use the file finder to show the contents of the CD. You will see two folders. Double-click on the *MacOS X* folder. Inside this folder is a program called *CogLab On A CD.jar*. (Depending on your system settings, you may or may not see the ending *.jar*) Double-click on this program. On MacOS X, the first window that you will see is the main window (next page).

MacOS 8.5-9.2

Use the file finder to show the contents of the CD. You will see two folders. Double-click on the *MacOS 8-9* folder. Inside this folder is a program called *CogLab On A CD*. Double-click on this program. You will see a window similar to the one shown above while the program is loading. Once it is loaded, you will see the main window (next page).

The CogLab Main Window

When the program has finished loading and is running, you will see a window similar to the one below (shown as it appears on Windows 98). This is the main CogLab window. From this window you can start any experiment, or view saved CogLab data files. Each button on the main window corresponds to an experiment. Click once on the button for the experiment that you want to complete.

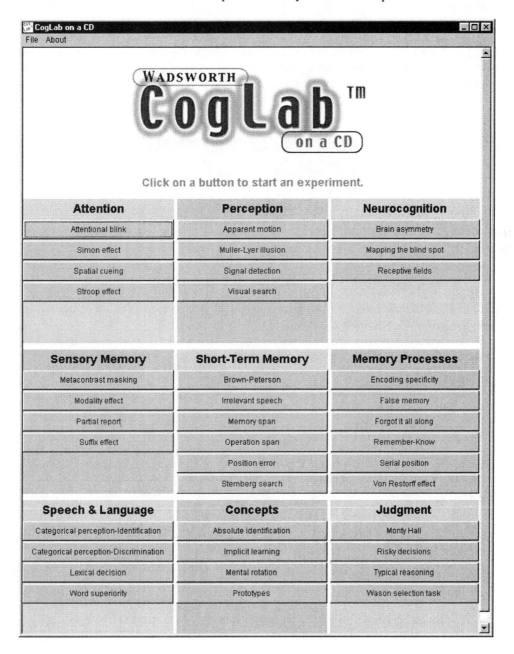

Running a CogLab Experiment

STEP 1: READ THE STUDENT MANUAL

First, read the instructions in the student manual for the experiment you want to run. The student manual provides background information about the experiment and provides instructions about how to do the experiment and how to interpret the results. Reading the instructions is very important, as each experiment works differently.

STEP 2: RUN THE EXPERIMENT

On the CogLab main window, find the button that corresponds to the experiment you want to run. Click once on this button. A new window (below) will appear that asks you to enter your first and last name. The names you enter will be included in the data that you generate. This embedding is useful if your instructor wants to verify that you completed assigned labs. After you enter your names, click on the *OK* button, or press the <return> key.

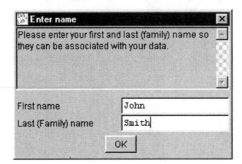

After you enter your names, an experiment window will appear. The graphic below shows the experiment window for the *Brown-Peterson* demonstration.

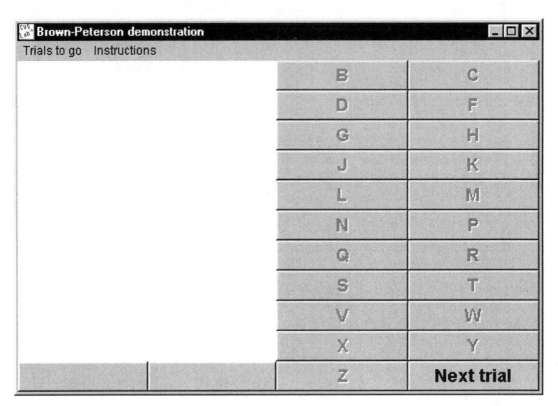

Every experiment window has two menus. Selecting the pull-down menu *Trials to go* shows how many trials remain in the experiment. As you proceed through the experiment, the trials to go will count down toward zero. You must complete all the trials in the experiment before you can see any results. If you stop the experiment before finishing, you will have to start over from the beginning.

The pull-down menu option *Instructions* opens a window with instructions on what you must do to start the next trial, what to observe during the trial, and what kind of responses are required. If the experiment involves key-presses, the instructions window may also allow you to change which keys are to be pressed.

STEP 3: SEE THE RESULTS

When you finish an experiment, the experiment window will close and shortly afterwards a summary of your data will appear. The graphic below shows typical results after completing the *Mental rotation* demonstration.

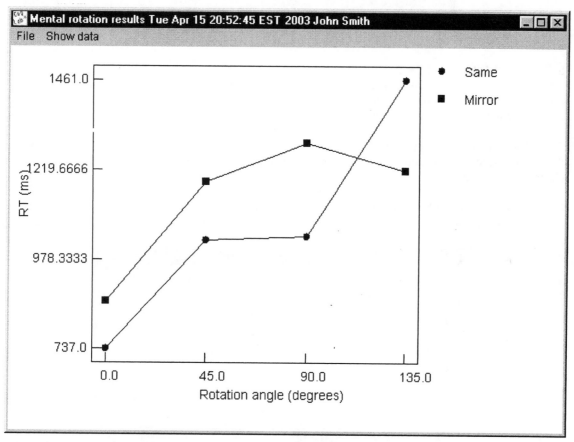

The menu option labeled *Show data* has two choices. Selecting menu item *Data summary* opens a new window with a tabular description of the results that are plotted in the graph. Selecting the menu item *Trial data* opens a new window that lists the conditions and responses of each trial in the experiment. This window also contains some information on how to interpret the experimental results.

Not every experiment summary shows a data plot. Some experiments show a table of data in a window. For example, the results of the *Stroop task* experiment are best shown as a data table (below) For a data table summary, the *Show data* menu only has the *Trial data* menu selection.

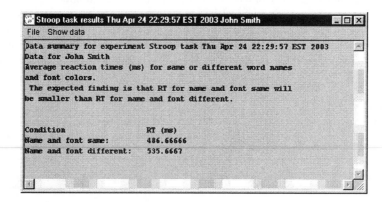

STEP 4: SAVE/PRINT THE RESULTS

After completing the experiment, you may want to print the results, import the data into a different program, or save the data for later analysis. Your instructor may also ask you to send him/her your saved data so that he/she can compile averages across your class.

The *File* menu on each results window provides methods for saving the data in three formats. By default the filename is always the name of the experiment appended to the name of the student, but this can be changed at the time of saving. (On MacOS 8-9, your name is *not* included in the file name.)

On Microsoft Windows 98-XP files will be saved to the My Documents folder by default, but you can also save the files to another folder with the file save window (below). Similar behavior holds for Mac OS.

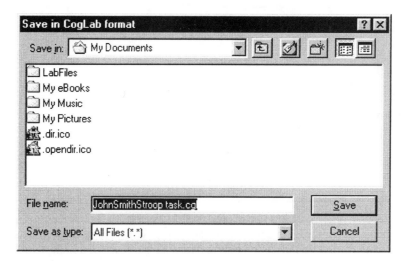

CogLab can save data in three different formats. Which format is most appropriate depends on what you want to do with the data.

CogLab format: This format preserves all the details of the CogLab results. The name you entered on step 2 is embedded in this format, along with the time that the experiment was finished. If your instructor wants you to send your results to him/her, this is probably the format he/she wants. Any file saved this way can be re-opened by CogLab using the *Open data in CogLab format* menu option under the *File* menu in the main CogLab window. This file will be saved with the extension *.cgl* so that it can be distinguished from other file types.

Plain text: This format saves only the textual parts of the results. It is useful primarily for importing the data into statistical packages that do not recognize the HTML format.

HTML: This format converts the results into an html document that can be viewed by a variety of programs including web browsers, MS Word, and MS Excel. Use this format to incorporate your results into other documents and to print the results. The easiest way to print data is to save it as an html file, open the file in a web browser such as Internet Explorer, and then use the print features of the web browser.

The graphic below shows the data for the *Mental rotation* experiment when it is saved as an HTML file and viewed in Internet Explorer.

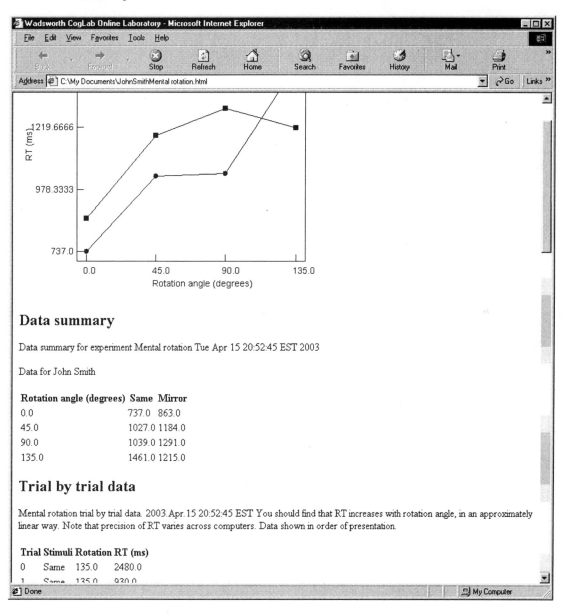

Data summary

Data summary for experiment Mental rotation Tue Apr 15 20:52:45 EST 2003

Data for John Smith

Rotation angle (degrees)	Same	Mirror
0.0	737.0	863.0
45.0	1027.0	1184.0
90.0	1039.0	1291.0
135.0	1461.0	1215.0

Trial by trial data

Mental rotation trial by trial data. 2003.Apr.15 20:52:45 EST You should find that RT increases with rotation angle, in an approximately linear way. Note that precision of RT varies across computers. Data shown in order of presentation.

Trial	Stimuli	Rotation	RT (ms)
0	Same	135.0	2480.0
1	Same	135.0	930.0

STEP 5: ADDITIONAL ANALYSIS

HTML data can also be easily imported into other programs for additional analysis. The graphic below shows CogLab data that was saved in HTML format and then imported into Microsoft Excel. The graph, formatting, and headers are all preserved. Significantly, each item in the tabular listings is given its own cell in the spreadsheet. This is useful for running further analyses on the trial-by-trial data.

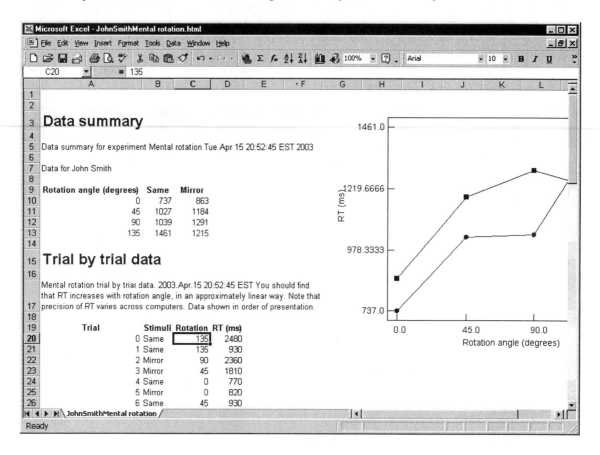

CogLab FAQ

FREQUENTLY ASKED QUESTIONS

Please see the *README.html* files on the CD for system specific information.

How much time does each experiment take?
Some experiments take only a few minutes whereas others can require nearly an hour. The Student Manual provides an estimate of the minimum time required to complete the experiment. You should allow an additional 5-10 minutes to read and understand the introduction and instructions, and an additional 5 minutes to contemplate the results. The estimated time does not include time for breaks.

Some experiments require a correct response on each trial. If you make many mistakes on these experiments, the experiment can take much longer.

Why doesn't the experiment begin?
If a window appears to start the experiment but nothing seems to happen, make certain that you are following the directions. Most experiments require you to press a key or click on a button to start an experimental trial. If the instructions ask you to press a key to start a trial, but nothing happens after the key press, click once in the middle of the window. Pressing the appropriate key should now produce a response from the window.

How do I print the data summary or graph?
Save the data in HTML format. Then open the saved file with a web browser. Use the printing capabilities of the web browser to print your data.

Why doesn't the "Trials to Go" menu count down?
Some experiments require that you provide a correct answer on each trial. When mistakes occur, the trial is repeated later in the experiment. If you never answer correctly, the *Trials to go* menu label properly shows that you have not completed any trials. Until you provide the correct answers for the trials the experiment *will not* end. Make sure you read the instructions for that experiment.

Why doesn't the window fill the entire screen?
Some experiments create a window that fills the entire screen, but not all of them do. The instructions indicate when that is to be expected.

I double-clicked on a data file saved in CogLab format, but CogLab didn't run; what happened?
Because *CogLab On A CD* is designed to be a cross-platform program, you cannot open a saved file by double-clicking on it. Instead, start the CogLab program and then select the *Open data in CogLab format* menu option under the *File* menu in the main CogLab window.

I'm running Windows 95 and an error occurs when I insert the CD; what's wrong?
The problem is with the auto run feature that starts up the program automatically when you insert the CD. *CogLab On A CD* doesn't officially support Windows 95. However, you can run *CogLab On A CD* manually on a Windows 95 computer by double-clicking on the program *COGLAB.exe*. You will not see the splash screen, and it is likely that it will take a minute or more for CogLab to load.

How do I get technical support?
If you purchased this CD new, you can obtain free technical support by calling 1-800-423-0563 or by emailing support@thomsonlearning.com. If you purchased this CD used, you are not eligible for technical support. Under the *About* menu item from the CogLab main window select the *Help* item for additional information on technical support.

Experiments

Attention – Attentional Blink

Cognitive mechanisms can handle only limited amounts of information. In many situations there are more stimuli and mental events than resources for processing. As a result, some stimuli are processed and some are not. The ability to selectively choose some stimuli and ignore others is called attention. Many studies of attention investigate how mental resources are switched from one stimulus to another. This experiment explores some properties of attention with rapidly changing stimuli. It shows that there is a brief time after paying attention to one stimulus where attention cannot be focused on a subsequent stimulus. This duration is called an attentional blink because it is analogous to being unable to see objects during an eye blink.

In the experiment many letters are shown in rapid succession, with each letter overwriting the previous letter. The observer's task is to watch the entire sequence, and then indicate whether certain target letters were in the sequence. The sequences are carefully constructed to systematically vary the temporal separation between two target letters. Thus, if the target letters are J and K, a sequence with the letters ". . . JXTVRK . . ." places K five letter-spaces beyond J.

The notable finding is that identification of the second target letter is very low when it quickly follows the first target letter. As temporal separation increases, identification of the second letter improves. This finding suggests that when the observer sees the first target letter he/she must attend to it to ensure that it will be remembered later. The focusing of attention to that letter apparently requires time, and if the second target letter appears during that time, it is not attended and not reported. By looking at recognition of the second letter as a function of separation, we can estimate the time required to focus and break attention for stimuli.

As a final note, although the task in this experiment may seem rather absurd, it is quite similar to tasks some individuals must perform on a routine basis. In the airline industry both pilots and controllers attend to many different stimuli that change characteristics very quickly. The temporal properties of attention revealed through studies like this one help guide development of more general theories of attention, with immediate applications to high-pressure situations. This experiment allows you to participate in a version of an attentional blink experiment.

Start a trial by pressing the space bar. A sequence of 19 letters will appear, with each new letter overwriting the previous one. Each letter is presented for only 100 milliseconds. Your task is to determine whether the letter J and/or K were in the sequence of letters just presented. You indicate the presence of a J by pressing the j key and you indicate the presence of the K by pressing the k key. If you see both letters, press each in any order. If you did not see either letter, do not press either key. The screen will present the key you press, but this is only so you know the program received your key press; it is not feedback on whether you were correct. When you are ready for the next trial, press the space bar again.

If for some reason you need to discard a trial (e.g., you sneezed, attention drifted, you "zoned out", et cetera) press the t key before pressing the space bar for the next trial. This will discard the just run trial (it will be re-run later in the experiment).

When you finish the experiment, a window will appear that plots the percentage of times you detected the first and second target letters as a function of separation. You should find that the second target is detected more frequently as separation increases. You should also find that the detection of the first target is relatively unaffected by separation. This finding supports the hypothesis that bringing attention to the first target interferes with detection of the second, but not vice-versa. A separation equal to zero corresponds to a sequence where only the first letter was presented. You should find that, for separation zero, detection frequency for the second target is zero. There are 100 trials in the experimental session. There are five letter separations, with 20 sequences for each separation. Each trial goes very quickly, so the experiment will probably not take more than half an hour. It will be a tiring half-hour, however, as you must apply yourself to the task of watching the rapid letter sequences.

Additional References

Arnell, K. M. & Jolicoeur, P. (1999). The attentional blink across stimulus modalities: Evidence for central processing limitations. *Journal of Experimental Psychology: Human Perception and Performance, 25*, 630-648.

Ross, N. N. & Jolicoeur, P. (1995). Attentional blink for color. *Journal of Experimental Psychology*: *Human Perception and Performance, 25*, 1483-1494.

Visser, T. A. W., Zuric, S. M., Bischof, W. F. & DiLollo, V. (1999). The attentional blink with targets in different spatial locations. *Psychonomic Bulletin and Review, 6*, 432-436.

Basic Questions

1. Assume that the theory of attentional blink is correct. Under that assumption, describe what the graph of percent reported vs. separation should look like for the first target and the second target.

2. Do your results look like what you described in question (1)? Explain why you have said "yes" or "no".

3. Use what you know about attentional blink to answer the following question: what two separate aspects of the stimulus presentation could you modify so that it would be easier to report the second target?

Advanced Questions

A. Use the plot of the mean percent detected as a function of separation to estimate how long an attentional blink lasts in this demonstration, (Hint: remember that each letter is presented for 100 milliseconds.)

Discussion Questions

1. The point has been made that attention is required to ensure that the first letter can be remembered later. What processes might be at work during an attentional blink? These processes would require attention and are for the purpose of making it possible to remember the first letter.

Attention – Simon Effect

The Simon effect refers to the finding that people are faster and more accurate responding to stimuli that occur in the same relative location as the response, even though the location information is irrelevant to the actual task (Simon, 1969). Studying the Simon effect gives us insight into a stage of decision making called "response selection." According to information processing theory, there are three stages of decision making: Stimulus identification, response selection and response execution or the motor stage.

Superficially, the Simon effect may seem similar to the Stroop effect. However, it is generally accepted that the interference that occurs in the Stroop effect comes from the stimulus identification, while the interference that occurs in the Simon effect occurs in the response selection stage. During response selection, a person uses a rule to translate the relevant stimulus dimension, usually shape or color, to the correct left or right response. However, the location dimension of the stimulus (its position on the screen) overlaps with the relevant stimulus dimension (left or right). Because of this, the irrelevant location dimension of the stimulus activates the corresponding response and interferes with making a response to the non-corresponding side. Because of this, same side responses are faster and more accurate than responses that are made opposite the location of the stimulus.

In the real world the Simon effect has important implications. Primarily, it shows that location information cannot be ignored, and will affect decision making, even if the user knows that the information is irrelevant. The Simon effect (and related phenomena) must be taken into account in design of man-machine interfaces. Good interfaces display information in ways that match the types of responses people should make. For example, imagine that you are flying a plane, and the left engine has a problem. The indicator for that engine should be to the left of a corresponding indicator for the right engine. If it is the other way around, you may misrespond to the indicator and adjust the wrong engine. That could be problematic.

After clicking on the start button, a window will appear to start the Simon effect experiment. Press the space bar to start the trial. A fixation dot will appear in the middle of the window, stare at it. A short time later (less than a second) you will be shown a red or green square on the left or right of fixation. Your task is to press the m key if the square is green and to press the v if the square is red. Keep your left index finger on the v, and your right index finger on the m. You will need to press the spacebar to start a new trial. After each trial, you will be given feedback whether your response was correct or incorrect, and how fast your reaction time was, in milliseconds.

After pressing the v or m key, press the space bar to start the next trial. If you wish, before pressing the space bar, but after pressing the v or m key, you can check how many trials remain for the current experiment with the pull-down menu.

There are 100 trials. You can discard a trial by pressing the t key instead of v or m. Discarding is appropriate if, after starting a trial, you sneeze, zone out, or are otherwise distracted. Discarded trials will be repeated later.

In every trial your goal is simply to press the m key if the square is green, and the v key if the square is red.

At the end of the experiment a table will appear that shows your mean reaction time for congruent and incongruent trials. A congruent trial is when the location of the square matched the location of the finger that you used to make the response (e.g., a green square requires a left hand response, so a congruent trial is one where the green square is on the left). Likewise an incongruent trial is one where the location of square is opposite the location of the finger used to make the response (e.g., a green square on the right). The expected result is that your reaction time will be faster for congruent than for incongruent conditions.

Additional References

De Houwer, J., Crombez, G., Baeyen, F. & Hermans, D. (2001). On the generality of the affective Simon Effect. *Cognition and Emotion, 15* (2), 189-206.

Hommel, B. (1995). S-R compatibility and the Simon Effect: Toward an empirical clarification. *Journal of Experimental Psychology: Human Perception and Performance, 21*, 764-775.

Ivanoff, J., Klein, R. & Lupianez, J. (2002). Inhibition of return with the Simon Effect: An omnibus analysis and its implications. *Perception & Psychophysics, 64* (2), 318-327.

Hommel, B. (1993). The role of attention for the Simon effect. *Psychological Research/Psychologische Forschung 55*, 208-222.

Kornblum, S., Hasbroucq, T., and Osman, A. (1990). Dimensional overlap: Cognitive basis for stimulus-response compatibility - A model and taxonomy. *Psychological Review*, 97, 253-270.

Miller, G.A., Galanter, E.& Pribram, K. (1960). *Plans and the structure of Behavior.* New York: Holt, Rinehate, & Winston.

Basic Questions

1. Both the Stroop and the Simon Effect seem like similar cognitive processes because reaction time slows down due to interference. What is the major difference between these 2 phenomenon?

2. After completing this lab you notice that you answer the desk phone with a different hand depending on which side the receiver cord is hanging down from. For example, if the phone cord is on the right side, you answer it with your right hand. How can you explain this behavior?

3. After buying a new stove, you find that you are continuously turning on the wrong elements. On this new stove, the controls for the elements are on the left-hand side and look like the picture below. Although there are pictures of the element that each button corresponds with, you are still having problems. Why are you having problems and how could you redesign your stove to help you?

4. You regularly miss the turnoff for your favorite restaurant, although you've been going there for the last 4 years. Until now you've always thought your sense of direction was bad. Although the restaurant is on the right hand side of the highway, the sign indicating the turnoff is on the left hand side (although it is a large sign). What do you suggest was your problem and how could the restaurant change the situation, so you don't miss the turnoff?

5. You injured your arm in a skiing accident and now you have it in a cast. Your psychology professor does not have a great deal of sympathy so she decides not to give you an extension on your major paper. You sit down to type out your essay, but it is awkward because you can only use 1 hand. If you injured your right arm, what word would take longer to type, "was" or "oil"? Explain your answer.

A. One of the car companies is introducing a new, wild-looking, futuristic car onto the market. It has a streamlined body, bucket seats and more buttons than you've ever seen in a car. It gets great gas mileage on the highway and in town. You notice that the rear bumper looks very different then you realize that the signal lights are positioned on the left-hand side of the bumper, just on the outside of the break lights. When they are activated, a large arrow flashes green for a left turn and red for a right turn. Although a large arrow is flashing and pointing in the direction of the turn, you still think they will be a problem. What kind of problems do you foresee?

B. Your little brother and his friend are playing a hand slapping game called, "Say Uncle". Person A holds their hands out in front of them, palms up while person B holds their hands directly over person A's, palms down. The person whose hands are on the bottom tries to slap the other person's hands as hard as possible in an attempt to get them to say "Uncle" or that they give up. Their opponent, however, has to try and remove their hands before getting hit. If the person evades a slap, they switch roles and they become the hitter. You notice that your brother is pretty fast slapping his friend's right hand with his right hand, but is slow (and usually misses) hitting his opponent's left hand with his right hand. What kind of advice should you give your brother?

C. As a way of decreasing bicycle/automobile collisions, the safety commissioner is trying to change the hand signals that cyclists give when they are turning. His logic is that the drivers can not see the hand signals in time, so they run into the bicycles. According to the Simon Effect, what would be a good start to changing the hand signals? Remember the goal is to decrease the reaction time by the motorists to the cyclists so they don't run into them.

Discussion Questions

1. As a runner, you've noticed that when oncoming drivers first spot you running on the road, they tend to steer their car towards you, but then they correct themselves and go around you. Discuss why you think this is happening and how you can do something about it?

2. How could a company that makes heavy equipment and machinery benefit from knowing about this cognitive phenomenon?

Attention – Spatial Cueing

The "spotlight" metaphor of visual attention nicely captures many characteristics of the focus of attention: it is a "beam" that is moved spatially, that may not be divided, and that enhances the detection of events falling within it.

Some of the strongest evidence supporting the unitary conception of attention comes from the luminance-detection paradigm (e.g., Posner, 1980). In such experiments, subjects are first cued with the likely spatial location of a target and then respond as rapidly as possible when the target appears at any location in the display. For example, in a typical display, the stimuli are arranged horizontally with a fixation point in the center, which is also the location where the cue appears. The cue is either valid, correctly identifying the spatial location of the target, or invalid, incorrectly identifying the location of the target. Following the presentation of the cue, a single target stimulus is illuminated (usually about 1000 ms after the onset of the cue) and subjects respond as soon as they detect the target, regardless of its location. Relative to a neutral cue condition, responses are faster when the target appears in the cued location (a valid trial) and slower when the target appears in a non-cued location (an invalid trial).

Demonstrations of these patterns of results occur independently of eye movements. In other words, when an eye tracker verifies that your eyes are still fixated on the center, your focus of attention can be off to the right, or off to the left. While other interpretations of these findings are possible, they are consistent with the notion of focused beam of attention that may be moved to distinct spatial locations - incorrectly in the case of the an invalid trial and correctly in the case of a valid trial.

After clicking on the start the button, a window will appear to start the experiment. Start a trial by pressing the space bar. A fixation dot will appear in the middle of the window; stare at it. A short time later a cue will appear. If the arrow points to the right, 80% of the time the target will appear on the right. If the arrow points to the left, 80% of the time, the target will appear on the left. If no arrow appears, the target is equally likely to appear on the left or right. A short time after the cue disappears, a red square will appear. Your task is to respond as quickly as possible when you see the square appear, regardless of its location. To respond, press the n key.

After pressing the n key, press the space bar to start the next trial. If you wish, before pressing the space bar, but after pressing the n key, you can check how many trials remain for the current experiment with the pull-down menu.

There are 80 trials. You can discard a trial by pressing the t key instead of n. Discarding is appropriate if, after starting a trial, you sneeze, zone out, or are otherwise distracted. Discarded trials will be repeated later.

In every trial your goal is simply to press the n key as soon as you see a red square appear.

At the end of the experiment a new window will appear that reports the reaction time in milliseconds for detecting the square in each of the conditions. The neutral condition provides a baseline measure when your attention is not cued. The expected result is that RTs in the valid condition (the arrow cue pointed to the correct location) will be faster than those in the neutral condition (a benefit) whereas RTs in the invalid condition (the arrow cue pointed to the wrong location) will be slower than those in the neutral condition (a cost).

7

Additional References

Atchley, P. & Kramer, A. (1998). Spatial cueing in a stereoscopic display: Attention remains "depth-aware" with age. *Journal of Gerontology: Psychological Sciences*, 53, 318-323.

Luck, S., Hillyard, S., Mouloua, M., Woldorff, M., Clark, V. & Hawkins, H. (1994). Effects of spatial cueing on luminance detectability: Psychophysical and electrophysiological evidence. *Journal of Experimental Psychology, Human Perception and Performance, 20*, 887-904.

Egly, R., Driver, J. & Rafal, R. D. (1994). Shifting visual attention between objects and locations:Evidence from normal and parietal lesion subjects. *Journal of Experimental Psychology: General, 123*, 161-177.

Eriken, C. W. & Yeh, Y (1985) *Allocation* of attention in the visual field. *Journal of Experimental Psychology: Human Perception and Performance, 11*, 583-597.

Posner, M. I. & Cohen, Y. (1984). Components of visual orienting. In H. Bouma & D. G. Bouwhuis (Eds.). *Attention and performance.* Hillside, NJ: Erlbaum

Basic Questions

1. When examining the results of the lab, which of the three reaction times were lower (faster) - (a) no cue (b) valid cue or (c) invalid cue? If the no cue reaction time was faster than the invalid cue, what could be inferred about invalid cues?

2. How does a ventriloquist use spatial cues to direct a person's attention away from him and towards his dummy or doll?

3. While exploring a cave, you hear screeching echoes that you believe are bats (not one of your favorite animals). What will happen to your reaction time if you try to escape the bats in this cave?

4. You are playing a video game where you place oddly shaped playing pieces into a game area as quickly as possible. The object is to form solid rows with these shapes to make the rows disappear because if there is a space, the row does not disappear. Just 0.5 seconds before a shape appears, a dot flashes on the side where it will come down from. However, as the game advances, you notice that sometimes the dots are on the wrong side as the shape. How do you think these miscues will affect your game?

5. You are playing your final game against York University, a strong offensive team. You are defending number 23, a top player and well known for his fancy footwork. Why does he beat you to the basket every time after he fakes his body to the right but then goes left? Explain in terms of your reaction speed to his moves.

Advanced Questions

A. In Classical Conditioning, effective learning of an association is diminished when the unconditioned stimulus and the conditioned stimulus are not paired closely together in time. How is this similar to something that could happen when presented with invalid cues?

B. How are cognitive expectations related to one's reaction time to a stimulus?

C. How might an animal, in its natural environment, use techniques to misinform a predator of its location?

Discussion Questions

1. How do you think directors of horror movies use invalid spatial cues to their advantage when the good guys are trying to get away from the bad guys (especially when a chainsaw is involved)?

2. In terms of conserving energy, why do animals, including humans, use heuristics or short cuts in cognitive tasks, since heuristics may be incorrect? When explaining your answer, think of this lab as well as others that you have done or other cognitive processes that you've talked about in class.

Attention – Stroop Effect

When you first learned to tie shoelaces you needed to carefully think through each step of the process. Now, you probably do not even seem to think about the steps, but simply initiate a series of movements that seem to proceed without any further influence. When a behavior or skill seems to no longer require direct interaction, cognitive psychologists say it is automatized.

Many behaviors can become automatized: typing, reading, writing, bicycling, piano playing, driving, etc. Automatization is interesting because it is an important part of daily life. We perform a variety of automatized behaviors quickly and effortlessly. In some cases people report that they do not consciously know how the behavior is performed, they just will it to happen, and it does happen.

To explore properties of automatized behaviors cognitive psychologists often put observers in a situation where an automatized response is in conflict with the desired behavior. This allows researchers to test the behind-the-scenes properties of automatized behaviors by noting their influence on more easily measured behaviors. This demonstration explores a well-known example of this type of influence, the Stroop effect.

Stroop (1935) noted that observers were slower to properly identify the color of ink when the ink was used to produce color names different from the ink. That is, observers were slower to identify red ink when it spelled the word blue. This is an interesting finding because observers are told to not pay any attention to the word names and simply report the color of the ink. However, this seems to be a nearly impossible task, as the name of the word seems to interfere with the observer's ability to report the color of the ink.

A common explanation for the Stroop effect is that observers (especially college undergraduates) have automatized the process of reading. Thus, the color names of the words are always processed very quickly, regardless of the color of the ink. On the other hand, identifying colors is not a task that observers have to report on very often, and because it is not automatized it is slower. The fast and automatic processing of the color name of the word interferes with the reporting of the ink color.

The Stroop task, and its many variations, is a commonly used tool in cognitive psychology to explore how different types of behaviors interact. This demonstration allows you to participate in a simple version of the Stroop task.

After clicking on the start the button, a window will appear to start the experiment. Start a trial by pressing the space bar. A fixation dot will appear in the middle of the window, stare at it. A short time later (less than a second) a word (RED, GREEN, or BLUE) will appear on the screen, and the word will be drawn in either red, green, or blue font color. Your task is to classify, as quickly as possible, the font color, regardless of the word name. If the font color is red, press the h key; for green, press the j key; for blue, press the k key. It may take a bit of practice to make certain you remember which key corresponds to which font color.

After pressing a key to identify the font color, you will receive feedback on whether you were correct. If you were incorrect the trial will be repeated later in the experiment. If you find you are making lots of mistakes you should slow down, or make certain you understood which key goes with which font color. Press the space bar to start the next trial. If you wish, before pressing the space bar, but after identifying the font color, you can check how many trials remain for the current experiment with the pull-down menu.

There are at least 45 trials, 30 where the font colors and word names are different, and 15 where the font colors and color names match (e.g., the word RED in red font color). You can also discard a trial by pressing the t key instead of identifying the font color. Discarding is appropriate if, after starting a trial, you sneeze, zone out, or are otherwise distracted. Discarded trials will be repeated later.

At the end of the experiment a new window will appear that reports the reaction time in milliseconds for identifying the font color when the word names and colors match and when they are different. You should find that the reaction time is longer when the word names and colors are different.

Additional References

Cohen, J. D., Dunbar, K. O., Barch, D. M. & Braver, T. S. (1997). Issues concerning relative speed of processing hypotheses, schizophrenic performance deficits, and prefrontal function: Comments on Schooler et al. (1997). *Journal of Experimental Psychology: General, 126,* 37-41.

MacLeod, C. (1997, March/April). Is your attention under your control? The diabolic Stroop effect. *Psychological Science Agenda,* pp. 6-7.

Williams, J. M. G., Mathews, A. & MacLeod, C. (1996). The emotional Stroop task and psychopathology. *Psychological Bulletin, 120,* 3-24.

Basic Questions

1. Identify the independent and dependent variables in this demonstration.

2. Imagine setting up a larger demonstration that uses all four of the following conditions for naming colors: color patches color words printed in conflicting ink colors color words printed in non-conflicting ink colors non-words printed in ink colors. Order the four conditions according to which will be the most difficult and which will be the easiest. "Difficult" means the reaction time will be long and "easy" means the reaction time will be short. Try to explain why you decided on this ordering.

3. Do you think that it might be possible to reduce the strength of the Stroop effect with some sort of practice? If "yes", what sort?

Advanced Questions

A. Use group mean reaction time for identifying font color when the word and the color match and group mean reaction time for identifying font color when the word and the color don't match to decide if the Stroop effect was confirmed in this demonstration.

Discussion Questions

1. Use what you know about automatic processing to explain the Stroop effect.

2. Suggest a variation on the Stroop effect using digits and asking participants to count them.

3. This demonstration measured reaction time. What other measures might be used to assess the Stroop effect?

Running Time: Minimum of 10 minutes. May be longer depending on the effort to find the find "best" motion percept.

Perception – Apparent Motion

If two stimuli are briefly flashed in rapid succession, observers will sometimes report seeing motion between the two stimuli. Reports of this type of apparent motion were investigated near the beginning of the 20th century by Gestalt psychologists (most notably Wertheimer). They noticed, among other things, that the timing of the flashes was important in determining whether or not motion was seen. If the time between the offset of the first stimulus and the onset of the second stimulus (called the interstimulus interval or ISI) is very short, observers simply see two dots presented nearly simultaneously. If the ISI is very long observers see one dot flash on and off and then the other flash on and off. For intermediate ISIs the first dot seems to turn off, move through the space between the dots and appear at the position of the second dot.

Korte (1915) noted that the ISI thresholds for seeing motion versus being too short varied with the spatial separation of the stimuli. The farther apart the stimuli were the longer the ISI needed to be for a good motion percept. This finding, and others, were formulated in a set of "Korte's laws" that have been used to describe aspects of apparent motion.

The relationship between spatial separation and ISI threshold is consistent with a variety of theories that hypothesize that the visual system builds a motion percept. For larger separations, the stimulus must "move" a farther distance, which presumably requires a greater length of time. This experiment allows you to see apparent motion in one of its simplest forms and to demonstrate Korte's law for yourself.

Apparent motion is the basis of movement in all television, movies, and computer animation. The screen actually shows a rapid succession of still images, the perceived motion is entirely "apparent" and illusory.

A window will fill the entire screen. Press the space bar key to start a trial. After pressing the space bar, a small fixation square will appear in the middle of the screen. Fixate this square. It will disappear after one and a half seconds. Half a second later a dot will appear on the right, disappear, and then a dot will appear on the left and disappear. These stimuli will then cycle back and forth repeatedly. Each of the dots is presented for 150 milliseconds; the duration of the blank between dots (the ISI) is variable.

Your task is to adjust the ISI until the motion percept is as strong as you can make it. You can increase the ISI by 20 milliseconds by pressing the i key. You can decrease the ISI by 20 milliseconds by pressing the k key. The ISI can never become negative.

After you are satisfied that the motion percept is as strong as you can make it, press the space bar to start the next trial. The spacing of the dots will vary from trial to trial. There are five spacings and five replications for each spacing for a total of 25 trials.

At the end of the experiment a graph will appear that plots the average Best ISI (in milliseconds) as a function of distance from the center of the screen (the number is the proportion of screen width). You should find that the Best ISI increases with distance. This would confirm some aspects of Korte's laws of apparent motion.

Additional References

Breitmeyer, B. G. (1984). *Visual masking: An integrative approach.* New York: Oxford University Press.

Ramachandran, V. S. & Anstis, S. M. (1986). The perception of apparent motion. *Scientific American, 254(6)*, 102-109.

Shiffrar, M. (1994). When what meets where. *Current Directions in Psychological Science, 3*, 96-100.

Basic Questions

1. Does your data confirm Korte's Law? Explain your answer.

2. Some people will find that their data doesn't confirm Korte's law. (You might even be one of them!) Suggest reasons that this might happen.

3. What type of graph do you think you would get if you used specific ISI's and adjusted the space between the dots? For each ISI you would be maximizing the perceived motion by adjusting the space between the dots.

Advanced Questions

A. Look at the plot of the mean best ISI's as a function of distance from the center. From these results decide if Korte's law is linear or curvilinear.

B. Compare the graph of your own data with the graph of the group data in (A). Which one shows a smoother relationship?

Discussion Questions

1. Explain how constructed "motion precepts" could be used to account for Korte's law. Do you think these precepts would operate at a conscious or unconscious level?

Perception - Muller-Lyer Illusion

This experiment serves two purposes. First, it introduces a well known perceptual illusion called the Muller-Lyer illusion. Second, it demonstrates a psychophysical experimental method called the method of constant stimuli.

The Muller-Lyer illusion is easily demonstrated. In the figure below there are three horizontal lines. Two of the lines contain a pair of "wings." The wings are drawn outward or inward from the line ends. The illusion is that the line with the outward drawn wings tends to look longer than the line with the inward drawn wings. The line without wings tends to look smaller than the line with outward drawn wings and bigger than the line with inward drawn wings. It is an illusion because the lines are actually all the same length, which you can verify with a ruler.

This experiment is not directly about experiencing the illusion, which can be done just by looking at the figure, but is about using the illusion to demonstrate a common experimental technique: the method of constant stimuli.

It is fun to look at visual illusions and realize how our perception differs from reality. To guide the development of theories on cognition and perception, however, we need more specific data. We need to know, for example, just how long does the line with the wings drawn outward look? The more general the question is, how do we measure characteristics of percepts? We cannot measure them directly because a percept is a particularly subjective experience.

The field of psychophysics deals with precisely this question. It attempts to relate reported characteristics of perception to physical properties. Instead of just asking an observer to look at and comment on stimuli, specific judgements are required and the stimuli are systematically varied. For the Muller-Lyer illusion, we will have observers compare the percept produced by a line with outward drawn wings to the percept produced by lines with no wings. We will systematically vary the length of the line without wings to see when the perceived line lengths match. We can then look at the physical length of the matching line without wings and use that as a measure of the strength of the Muller-Lyer illusion. There are several ways to go about making such comparisons. One of the simplest and most powerful is the method of constant stimuli. We will generate a large set of lines without wings of varying lengths and have the observer compare each one with a standard line with wings. For each comparison the observer notes whether the line without wings is perceived to be bigger or smaller than the line with wings. Unlike some other psychophysical methods (like the method of adjustment), the stimuli are not changeable by the observer, thus they are constant stimuli. The observer's task is just to report on the percept.

The goal of this type of experiment is to produce a psychometric function. That is a set of values that describes the probability of a certain response as a physical characteristic is varied. For the Muller-Lyer experiments, we will find the proportion of reports where the line without wings seemed bigger than the standard as a function of the physical length of the line without wings. With such a curve you can often identify critical values, such as the point of subjective equality, where the line without wings seemed to be the same size as the line with wings (e.g., 50% of the time it is described as bigger and 50% of the time is described as smaller).

A window will fill the entire screen. Press the space bar key to start a trial. After pressing the space bar, two vertical lines will appear. The line on the lower right has outward drawn wings. The line on the upper left has no wings. Your task is determine whether the line without wings is bigger or smaller than the line with wings. Press the i-key if the line without wings seems longer than the line with wings. Press the k-key if the line without wings seems shorter than the line with wings. Text will appear near the center of the screen with each keypress to indicate that the computer has received your response. You can change your response if you wish. When you are satisfied with your response, press the space bar key to then start the next trial.

There are a total of 225 trials. Each trial only takes a few seconds to complete. Do not go too fast, though, or the computer will tell you to slow down and take time to make an accurate judgement of relative line lengths.

At the end of the experiment a graph will appear that plots the proportion of "Bigger" responses for different lengths of test lines (without wings). This is an approximation of the psychometric function. You should find that the proportion is zero on the far left of the plot and smoothly rises to the value one on the far right of the plot. On the y-axis find the location of the 0.5 mark. Go straight across horizontally to the plotted curve. Then go straight down to the x-axis. The length (in pixels) there is the perceived length of the line with wings. You should find that the number is larger than 100 (the actual length of the line with wings). That the number is larger than 100 is a quantitative description of the magnitude of the Muller-Lyer illusion.

Additional References

Coren, C. & Girgus, J. S. (1978). *Seeing is deceiving: The psychology of visual illusions.* Hillsdale, NJ: Erlbaum.

Coren, S., Porac, C., Aks, D. J. & Morikawa, K. (1988). A method to assess the relative contribution of lateral inhibition to the magnitude of visual geometric illusions. *Perception and Psychophysics, 43,* 551-558.

Gregory, R. L. (1966). *Eye and brain* (3rd ed.) New York: McGraw-Hill.

Segall, M. H., Campbell, D. T. & Herskovits, M. J. (1966). *The influence of culture on perception.* Indianapolis: Bobbs-Merrill.

Basic Questions

1. Do your data confirm the Muller-Lyer illusion?

2. What is "constant" in the method of constant stimuli for this demonstration?

3. If the point of subjective equality came out to be less than 100 pixels, how would you interpret what happened?

Advanced Questions

A. Using the group psychometric function, find the point of subjective equality for the group data. Does it confirm the Muller-Lyer illusion?

Discussion Questions

1. If you were to use the method of constant stimuli but this time using the inward pointing wings, what would be the result?

Perception - Signal Detection

Much of cognitive psychology involves gathering data from experimental participants. Gathering good data is not always easy, especially when one uses a variety of people as participants. Researchers often must carefully design an experiment to be certain participants are following the instructions and are motivated to try their best. Even despite these efforts, experimental results can be contaminated by individual differences if the researcher does not properly analyze the data.

For example, consider two participants in visual detection of a faint target. The researcher wants to explore a property of the visual system, so he/she presents a visual stimulus and asks the participants to report whether they saw the target. After 50 trials, participant A reports seeing the target 25 times and participant B reports detection 17 times. Did participant A do better? Not necessarily, perhaps participant A is simply more prone to report seeing the target and participant B is more conservative. That is, the two participants may have equivalent visual systems, but differences in reporting. Reports of simple detection do not allow the researcher to compare participants' results.

A better experiment is a modification of the one above. Have two kinds of trial, one with the target present and one with the target absent. Again have subjects report whether they saw the target. There are four statistics to be calculated from this experiment. Trials where a participant correctly detects the target are called hits. The trials where the target was there but participants did not detect it are called misses. If a participant reports seeing the target when it was not actually there, he/she has made a mistake (false alarm). A trial where the participant correctly reports that the target was not present is a correct rejection.

Suppose that after 100 trials (50 for target present and 50 for target absent) the researcher again finds that on the trials where the target was in fact present, participant A reports seeing it 25 times and participant B 17 times. Who is doing better? It depends on the frequency of false alarms. If participant A has 25 false alarms and participant B has 5 false alarms, then B is better than A at distinguishing the trials where the target is present from the trials where the target is absent. That is, in this case, A seems to often guess that the target is there, but he/she is wrong (false alarm) as often as right (hit). B is more selective about saying he/she detects the target, but rarely says the target is there when it is not. Thus, B is doing better.

This type of analysis suggests that you need to consider two numbers, hits and false alarms to really be able to compare performance across subjects. Fortunately, one can combine the numbers in a careful way to produce a single number that gives an indication of the sensitivity of the participant to the presence of the target. The calculation is structured so that, with certain assumptions, it will not matter whether a participant takes a conservative or liberal approach to claiming to detect the target. There are two measures of sensitivity that are often used. One is called d' (d-prime) and is based on signal detection theory. The other is called log(alpha) and is based on choice theory. For most situations the two measures give very similar results, although there are quantitative differences.

A discussion of the algorithms for calculating sensitivity is beyond the scope of this experiment [see Macmillan & Creelman, (1991) for further discussion]. Instead, you will participate in an experiment that measures sensitivity.

After clicking on the start button, a window will appear that fills the screen. Press the space bar to start a trial. After pressing the bar a fixation point will appear for a second or so and then will be replaced by randomly placed dots (sort of like a "star field"). On some trials (target present) an additional set of ten dots arranged in a straight line that slants downward from left to right is randomly placed among the dot field. On the other trials (target absent), the line is not included. Your task is to report whether the target is present or absent.

If you think the target is present, press the / key. If you think the target is not present, press the z key. You will be given feedback on whether you were correct. In addition, on the trials where the target was actually present, a green line will connect the target dots after you make your decision. Look for the dots along this line so you will learn what the target looks like; but the target will be randomly placed on the screen from trial to trial. There are a total of 60 trials. Thirty with the target line present and thirty with the target line absent.

When the experiment finishes the window will close and a new window will appear with data on your performance. The data will include several statistics:
- HITS: the percentage of times you said you detected the target and it was actually there.
- FALSE ALARMS: the percentage of times you said you detected the target, but the target was not actually present.
- CORRECT REJECTIONS: the percentage of times you said you did not detect the target, and the target was not actually present.
- MISSES: the percentage of times you said you did not detect the target, but it was actually there.

The data will also report a sensitivity statistic called d' (pronounced dee-prime). The program uses a method proposed by Brophy (1986) to compute d'. The larger the d' value, the better your performance. A sensitivity value of zero means that you cannot distinguish trials with the target from trials without the target. A sensitivity of 4.6 indicates a nearly perfect ability to distinguish between trials that included the target and trials that did not include the target. Values between these extremes correspond to intermediate sensitivity to the target. (Negative sensitivities are possible, but will be close to zero unless you misunderstood the instructions.) You will also see the signal detection measure of response bias, C (see Snodgrass & Corwin, 1988). A value greater than 0 indicates a conservative bias (a tendency to say 'absent' more than 'present') and a value less than 0 indicates a liberal bias. Values close to 0 indicate neutral bias.

You can repeat the experiment several times, and intentionally vary your approach to making responses. For one experiment you could take a very conservative approach and only report that you see the target if you are very certain. One another session of the experiment you could take a looser approach and report that you see the target unless you are certain it is not there. You should find that your sensitivity score does not change very much, even though your bias score will vary substantially.

Additional References

Dai, H., Versfeld, N. J. & Green, D. M. (1996). The optimum decision rules in the same-different paradigm. *Perception and Psychophysics, 58,* 1-9.

Green, D. M. & Swets, J. A. (1974). *Signal detection theory and psychophysics* (reprint). New York: Kreiger. (Original work published 1966).

Swensson, R. G. (180). A two-stage detection model applied to skilled visual search by radiologists. *Perception and Psychophysics, 27,* 11-16.

Basic Questions

1. If you were to go through this demonstration again, but this time you were told that there would be only 15 trials in which the line was present and 45 trials in which it was absent, what would happen to your percentage of hits and false alarms?

2. With the same conditions as in question (1), what would happen to your sensitivity [or your log(alpha)]?

3. A friend just did the signal detection demonstration and she wants to compare her results with yours. Unfortunately she just happened to delete the percentage of hits and false alarms from her data and now she has only the percentage of misses and correct negatives. How can she reconstruct what the percentages of hits and false alarms were?

Advanced Questions

A. Using the group data supplied to you by your instructor, arrange participants from most sensitive to least sensitive. What happens to participant hits and false alarms as sensitivity increases?

B. Using the group data supplied to you by your instructor, arrange participants from most liberal to most conservative. What happens to participant hits and false alarms as participant range from liberal to conservative?

Discussion Questions

1. What happens to the hit and false alarm rate as a participant becomes more liberal? More conservative?

Perception – Visual Search

This experiment explores aspects of attention in a visual search task. It is a classic experiment that makes strikingly clear the time needed to bring attention to bear on different regions of visual space. The basic idea is to ask a participant to search a visual image for a particular item and to respond as quickly as possible once they find the item, or to respond as quickly as possible when they are certain the item is not in the image. This type of experiment was used to develop a popular theory of attention (Treisman & Gelade, 1980).

Searches are divided into two types, those that require selective use of attention and those that do not. In the latter, the target item seems to "pop out" of the display and the participant can respond quickly. Notably, this pop out effect allows the participant to respond quickly even when the number of other (distractor) items is increased. In the other type of displays it seems that the participant is forced to study each item individually until the target item is found. In these cases the target item does not pop out, and search time increases with the number of distractor items. Controlling whether attention is needed or not is accomplished by the type of target and distractor items. In the experiment below, the target is always a green circle. For the feature condition the distractors are always blue squares. As you will see, the green circle seems to pop out of the image to quickly identify the location of the target. To require attention, the distractor items are made more complex. Some of the distractors are green squares while others are blue circles. Because some of the distractors are green, the green target circle no longer pops out and the participant must search through all the items to find the one that is both green and a circle. This type of search is a called conjunctive search because the target is a conjunction of features in the distractors.

After clicking on the start button, a window will appear to start the feature search experiment. After positioning the mouse in the window press the space bar. A fixation dot will appear in the middle of the window, stare at it. A short time later (less than a second) circles and squares of various colors will appear on the screen. Your task is to determine if there is a green circle among the shapes. When you see a green circle, press the / key on your keyboard as quickly as possible. When you are certain there is not a green circle in the window, press the z key on your keyboard, again as quickly as possible.

After pressing the z or / key, press the space bar to start the next trial. If you wish, before pressing the space bar, but after pressing the z or / key, you can check how many trials remain for the current experiment with the pull-down menu.

The feature and conjunctive trials consist of approximately 48 trials each. If you make a mistake (e.g., say "Present" when you should have said "Absent") that trial is repeated later in the experiment, so you may actually run more than 48 trials. You can also discard a trial by pressing the t key instead of z or /. Discarding is appropriate if, after starting a trial, you sneeze, zone out, or are otherwise distracted. Discarded trials will be repeated later.

In every trial your goal is simply to determine if a green circle is present. If it is press /, if it is not press z. If you are frequently incorrect (feedback is given when you are incorrect), try to delay your response until you are more certain that you are correct.

After you finish the set of feature search trials, the window will close and a new window will appear to present the conjunctive search trials.

After running both experiments a plot will appear that shows the time required for you to find the target ("Present" condition) or realize that the target was not there ("Absent" condition). These times will be plotted against "Number of distractors", which is the number of items on the screen. You should find that for the feature conditions changes in the number of distractors has little effect on search time. For the conjunctive searches you should find that search times increase with the number of distractors. You should also find that conjunctive "Absent" searches increase with the number of distractors at a faster rate than the conjunctive "Present" searches.

Additional References

Palmer, S. E. (1999). *Vision science: Photons to phenomenology*. Cambridge, MA: MIT Press.

Treisman, A. (1993). The perception of features and objects. In A. Baddeley and L. Weiskrantz (Eds.), *Attention: Selection, awareness, and control*. Oxford, England: Clarendon.

Treisman, A. & Sato, S. (1990). Conjunction search revisited. *Journal of Experimental Psychology: Human Perception and Performance, 16,* 459-478.

Basic Questions

1. Suppose that you decided to keep the number of distracters in this demonstration constant at 64. *According to our understanding of visual search processes*, predict what would be the easiest condition, the next most difficult condition, the next most difficult condition after that, and the most difficult condition. The conditions are: feature present, conjunctive present, feature absent, conjunctive absent. (Hint: "difficult" means that the reaction time is long.)

2. Do your data correspond with what you predicted in question (1)?

3. Use what you know about visual search to predict which of each pair would be easier to search for:
    the letter 0 among V's or the letter P among R's and Q's
    a lime among lemons and medium sized dill pickles or a lemon among bananas

Advanced Questions

A. Using the group data supplied to you by your instructor, calculate the mean reaction time for each different number of distractors over all four conditions.

B. Using the data from (A) plot four lines—conjunctive absent, conjunctive present, feature absent, feature present—making the reaction time a function of the number of distractors.

C. Do the data in (B) confirm the difference between conjunctive and feature searches?

Discussions Questions

1. What processes might be at work to make feature searches fast (and not Requiring attention) and conjunctive searches slow (and requiring attention)?

2. Explain why conjunctive absent searches should increase as a faster rate with number of distractors than conjunctive present searches.

Neurocognition – Brain Asymmetry

You may have heard that each person has two distinct hemispheres of the brain, with different capabilities. For example, the sensory signals from the left side of your body are sent to the right hemisphere of your brain; and the sensory signals from the right side of your body are sent to the left hemisphere of your brain. Likewise, control of your right arm and leg is via your left hemisphere; and control of your left arm and leg is via your right hemisphere. More notable cognitive differences also exist. The left hemisphere is said to deal with language and analytical thought, while the right hemisphere is said to deal with spatial relations and creativity. The basis for these claims about cognition comes from investigations of clinical patients who, usually to control a serious case of epilepsy, underwent a surgery that separated their left and right hemispheres. (This surgery prevented epileptic seizures from passing from one hemisphere to the other.) Careful studies of these split-brain patients revealed fascinating properties about how the brain was organized. A patient asked to fixate on a spot on a screen could verbally report words flashed on the right side of the screen (those words were sent to the left hemisphere). The patient could not say the word if it was flashed on the left side of the screen (thus sent to the right hemisphere). Notably, the patient could identify, by picking up with the left hand a physical item matching a word flashed on the left side of the screen.

Subsequent work showed a variety of differences between the brain hemispheres, and some researchers concluded that even people without split brains effectively have two competing brains. These conclusions were picked up by the popular press, and one now sees a variety of claims that schools should nurture one brain side instead of another, or that different types of therapy should be used to strengthen an undeveloped hemisphere.

Some of these claims appear in very odd places. For example, unrelated research suggests that Mozart's music stimulates creativity and intelligence in children. One CD jacket claims that Mozart's music stimulates the left-brain to improve logical skills. It suggests positioning the speakers on the child's right side (presumably so the sound goes to the left brain). It is nice music and may help improve logical skills, but the left-brain, right-brain difference does not necessarily have anything to do with it. Moreover, sound will go in both ears and reach both hemispheres, so positioning the speakers on one side versus another cannot possibly make much difference.

As it turns out, it is rather difficult to find much difference at all between the two hemispheres in normals (individuals without split-brain surgery). This is not to suggest that there are no differences, but the functional significance of these differences may be very slight. Moreover, when such differences do exist, they tend to be strongest for right-handed males. Females and left-handed individuals tend to not show brain-side effects nearly as well.

This experiment lets you search for differences between your left and right hemispheres. It is an unusual experiment in that it is quite possible that you will not find an effect. Given the pervasive nature of the left-brain, right-brain belief, however, a person knowledgeable about cognitive psychology should recognize how difficult it can be to demonstrate such effects.

Your task is to categorize stimuli as quickly as possible. Stimuli will be words or shapes. The stimuli will appear on either the left side of the display (and thus go to your right hemisphere) or on the right side of the display (and thus go to your left hemisphere). If the left hemisphere is really more strongly involved in language processing, you might expect that words presented on the right side of the screen will be responded to faster than words presented on the left side of the screen. Likewise, shapes presented to the left side of the screen might be responded to faster because they are sent to the right hemisphere, which deals with spatial and geometrical information.

The demonstration is split into two experiments that are run in succession. Start by clicking on the button below. A window will appear. After positioning the mouse in the window, press the space bar. A fixation dot will appear in the middle of the window, stare at it and make a concerted effort to not move your eyes during an experimental trial. One to two seconds later a green shape will appear, either on the right or the left side of the screen. Your task is to determine whether the shape is a circle (press the / key) or a square (press the z key). You will be given feedback on whether your classification was correct. After pressing the z or / key, press the space bar to start the next trial.

There are at least 80 shape classifications to be made, with equal numbers of shapes and sides of presentation. It should not concern you which side of the screen the shape is drawn. Simply note whether the shape is a circle or a square.

After running the shape experiment, the program will immediately start to run an experiment involving the classification of words. The word stimuli are all verbs and your task is to classify each verb as present or past tense. The present tense words are FALL, RUN, SEE, SHOOT, WRITE. The past tense words are FELL, RAN, SAW, SHOT, WROTE. You are to respond as quickly as possible whether the current word is present tense (press the / key) or past tense (press the z key). In other respects the experiment is similar to the shape experiment.

Gathering good data for this experiment requires that you become quite good at the classification experiment. There are at least 160 trials. If you incorrectly classify a stimulus, it will be presented again later. If you make mistakes often, slow down to ensure that you apply yourself to the classification task. You may find that you need to run this experiment several times to get good at the classification task. If you wish, before pressing the space bar, but after pressing the z or / key, you can check how many trials remain for the current experiment with the pull-down menu. You can also discard a trial, if you are distracted during its presentation, by pressing the t key instead of the z or / key. A discarded trial will be repeated later in the experiment. Remember to keep your eyes focused on the fixation point throught a trial. Do not move them to look at the shape or word, doing so will invalidate the experiment.

After the experiment a window will appear that summarizes your results. The data gives the average reaction time (RT) for four conditions: Shape left, Shape right, Word left, and Word right. Left and right correspond to the location of the stimulus on the screen, so the corresponding hemisphere in your brain is the flip (e.g., Left location -> Right hemisphere). Strong evidence for brain asymmetry would be found if Shape left RT was smaller than Shape right RT and Word left RT was larger than Word right RT. Not finding this type of data does not necessarily mean there is no asymmetry, but the statistical calculations needed to draw the conclusion are more complicated. The tests needed to test for brain asymmetry in those cases can be calculated using the trial-by-trial data.

Additional References

Gazzaniga, S. & LeDoux, J. E. (1978). *The integrated mind.* New York: Plenum Press.

Sperry, R. W. (1966). Brain bisection and consciousness. In J. Eccles (Ed.), *Brain and consciousness experience.* New York: Springer-Verlag.

Springer, S. P. & Deutsch, G. (1998). *Left brain, right brain: Perspectives from cognitive neuroscience* (5th ed.). New York: W. H. Freeman.

Basic Questions

1. Does your data support the idea that the brain is asymmetric? Explain your answer.

2. In this demonstration there is more practice provided for word conditions than for shape conditions. How might this affect the data?

3. Suppose a split brain patient were to do this demonstration. Would the results be different? Why or why not?

Advanced Questions

A. Use the group mean reaction times for each of 4 conditions: shape left location, shape right location, word left location, word right location to decide if brain asymmetry is confirmed in this demonstration.

Discussion Questions

1. Suggest some specific cognitive processes that might underlie right brain/left brain differences.

Neurocognition – Mapping the Blind Spot

The back of each of your eyes contains a dense set of receptors that are sensitive to light energy. These receptors convert light energy into electrical energy, which eventually is transferred to your nervous system and your brain. These receptors, however, are not distributed evenly across your eye. There is a central location, called the fovea, where the receptors are very densely packed. Generally, when you stare at an object you are arranging your eyes so that the object's image falls on the foveae of your eyes. Outside the fovea there are fewer receptors. In fact, in some places there are no receptors at all.

There is a place in each eye where the optic nerve exits the back of the eye to send information to the brain. This "hole" is called the optic disk. It contains no light sensitive receptors. As a result, any light that falls on this part of the eye is undetected and invisible to you. Functionally, this location on the eye is called the blind spot.

You have probably never noticed your blind spots (one in each eye). This is for several reasons. First, each blind spot is far away from its eye's fovea. Because the fovea is typically where you are "looking," you would not generally notice that something has disappeared into a blind spot. Second, when you view the world with two eyes, one eye can compensate for the other eye's blind spot. Light that falls into the blind spot of one eye generally does not fall on the blind spot of the other eye. Third, your brain only processes the presence of information, not the absence. Your brain does not notice a "hole" in the information it receives from the eye. It simply works with the information it receives. In a similar way, the brain does not observe that we are unable to view ultraviolet light. It has no knowledge about "missing" information.

With the proper experiment, however, it is possible to identify and map the blind spot which is the purpose of this experiment. You will probably be surprised at how large the blind spot is. It covers a large part of your visual field. The experiment used here is similar to a test used by eye doctors to identify visual scotomas (damaged spots in the retina of your eye). Should you consistently find "holes" in your data other than the blind spot, you may want to see an eye doctor.

A window will fill the entire screen. A small blue fixation square will be on the far left of the screen. The experiment is designed to map the blind spot of your right eye. Close your left eye (or cover it with your hand or a patch). Fixate the small square with your right eye. Try to sit so that your head is centered directly in front of the fixation square. Press the space bar key to start a trial. A dot will appear somewhere on the screen. Your task is to report whether you see the dot or not, all while keeping your right eye fixated on the small blue square.

If you see the dot, press the m-key. If you do not see the dot, press the n-key. Either of the keys you press will produce written feedback at the location of the fixation point. This is simply to indicate that the computer received your response. If the response is not what you intended (e.g., you pressed m when you meant to press n), just press the intended key. The computer will keep your last response as the response for that trial. Do not move your eye from the fixation square when you make this judgment. Press the space bar key to start the next trial when you are ready.

There are a total of 300 trials. That may sound like a lot, but each trial takes only a couple of seconds. You can take a break if you wish, but try to stay seated in the same position when you resume the experiment. If you move around, your blind spot will also move with you and the data will be a mix of the two positions you take. Also, be careful to make accurate judgments of whether you see or do not see the dot. If you try to go too fast, the computer will warn you to slow down. Most importantly, keep your right eye fixated on the small blue square. If you move your eye around, be sure to go back to the fixation square before making your judgment about seeing or not seeing a dot.

At the end of the experiment, you will be given two forms of data. First, the experimental window will show a full array of dots colored green and red. These dots are in the same locations you just viewed during the experiment. Any dot colored green is one that you reported as visible. Any dot colored red is one that you reported as not visible. You should find that there is a patch of red dots near the middle of the array. These are dots whose image fell on the blind spot of your eye. Its precise location varies a bit among observers and varies a lot depending on how far you are seated from the monitor. The same data is also presented in a data table in a separate window. Here 1's and 0's are used to indicate seen and not seen dots in the array, respectively.

Additional References

Brown, R. J. & Thurmond, J. B. (1993). Preattentive and cognitive effects on perceptual competition at the blind spot. *Perception and Psychophysics, 53,* 200-209.

Ramachandran, V. S. (1992). Blind spots. *Scientific American, 266,* 86-91.

Sergent, J. (1988). An investigation into perceptual completion in blind areas of the visual field. *Brain, 111,* 347-373.

Basic Questions

1. Try to interpret your data. Did you find a blind spot? One or more than one? Is it (are they) clearly defined or fuzzy?

2. What would visual perception be like if you saw the world with only one eye and simulation sometimes fell on the blind spot?

3. What would visual perception be like if we had no blind spots at all?

Advanced Questions

A. Transfer the group data generated by the program onto acetate transparency sheets. This will allow you to compare participants' blind spot maps.

B. Try to assess the amount of variability in number, location, size, and clarity of blind spots across participants.

Discussion Questions

1. Not everyone will obtain blind spots that are the same size or in the same location. Suggest some reasons why this might happen.

Neurocognition – Receptive Fields

A fundamental tenet of cognitive science is that the mind can be understood by studying the brain. The brain consists of billions of individual cells (neurons), whose combined behavior corresponds to what we call cognition. Because of the immense number of neurons and their complicated connections, it is difficult to relate the behavior of an individual neuron with human behavior (e.g., seeing a red apple).

A concept that helps make that connection, in certain cases, is the receptive field. Basically, the receptive field of a neuron consists of any stimulus that changes the neuron's firing rate. By definition, every neuron has a receptive field, although the receptive fields for some neurons are very complicated. The concept of a receptive field is most useful in those parts of the brain that are tied to specific senses (e.g., touch, audition, vision, taste) or to motor control. For neurons sensitive to visual information, for example, the receptive field describes how spatial patterns of light influence the neuron's behavior. It is often the case that a neuron responds only when light falls within a certain part of the visual field. Moreover, the light can have excitatory or inhibitory effects, depending on where it falls in the receptive field. Identifying the region of the receptive field and the excitatory and inhibitory parts provides a good deal of information about the role of the neuron in visual perception.

In a neurophysiological study of visual receptive fields (and there are many), a researcher typically inserts an electrode into a neuron to record its electrical potential (including action potentials). The researcher then presents visual stimuli to the animal and records the cellular responses. By noting changes in the electrical potential (or in the number of action potentials), the researcher can determine if light at a particular location is: (a) excitatory, (b) inhibitory, or (c) outside the receptive field and thus neither excitatory nor inhibitory. By carefully watching the cell's behavior as the stimulus changes, the researcher can map out the receptive field of a neuron.

Knowledge about neural receptive fields is of great significance for understanding perception. For example, neurons close to the retinas of your eyes have (relatively) circularly shaped receptive fields. For some neurons the center of this circle is excitatory, while the surround is inhibitory. Other neurons switch the locations of excitation and inhibition. Some neurons in area V1 of the cortex are sensitive to light-to-dark edges of a specific orientation. Other neurons in area V1 are sensitive to light-to-dark edges but are also sensitive to dark-to-light edges of the same orientation. The properties of these neurons play a fundamental role in theories of visual perception.

This experiment provides you with the opportunity to map out receptive fields. Your task is to find the receptive field, partly identify its excitatory and inhibitory regions, and categorize the neuron based on its receptive field properties. Do not take the properties of the virtual neurons too literally. The receptive fields are caricatures of true receptive fields; they do not take into account much of the underlying neurophysiology. This caveat aside, this experiment will hopefully introduce you to the concept of receptive fields.

Clicking on the practice or experiment buttons below will initiate the different parts of the experiment. A window will appear with three basic components. On the bottom left is a drawing canvas. Here you draw images that are to be presented to the virtual visual system. On the top left is a plot that shows the response of the cell to the most recently submitted image. On the right are checkboxes and buttons for you to guess the neuron category, start the next trial, change the drawing color, submit an image to the virtual visual system, clear the drawing canvas, and show the actual receptive field of the cell.

Your task is to draw a stimulus that generates a response in the neuron that is at least 50% of its maximal response. Once you have that stimulus you can guess the category and move on to the next trial. When you correctly guess the category you can also click on a button to show the true shape of the receptive field.

The practice version is just like the experiment version, except you can always reveal the true shape of the receptive field by clicking on the Show RF button. It is a good idea to start with the practice version because it allows you to see the receptive field and explore how light patterns correspond to electrical potentials. A shown receptive field is represented on the drawing canvas by a green (excitatory) region and a red (inhibitory) region. The locations of the green and red pixels correspond to the location in visual space of the receptive field. With the mouse, click in the middle of the green region and then click on the Submit image button. You should see that the plot of electrical potential shows a small hill. Each image submission corresponds to presenting the drawn image (not the red and green, only what you draw) to the virtual animal for 300 milliseconds. The electrical potential rises at stimulus onset (time zero) and falls after stimulus offset (time 300 ms). The spikes plotted intermittently correspond to action potentials. Action potential frequency increases as electrical potential increases, but action potentials can also occur without a stimulus.

Try filling in more and more of the green region with white blocks. When you click on the Submit image button you should find that the neuron gives a stronger and stronger response. Now start filling in some of the red region as well. You will find that the electrical potential is smaller and there are fewer action potentials. When you fill in all of the red and the green you should find that the neuron does not respond to the stimulus any differently than it responds to a blank screen.

You can clear the white you have drawn in two ways. One way is to click on the Clear image button. This clears the screen of everything. The second way is to click on the Draw in black button. This changes the drawing color so that it will draw black squares instead of white squares (it is like a small eraser). Clicking on Draw in white button will return the mouse control to drawing in white again.

Keep exploring with different light patterns until you think you have a pretty good idea how to use the controls and how different light patterns change the neuron's behavior. Draw and submit an image that generates a strong response from the neuron. Click on the checkboxes. A message will appear indicating when you are correct in your categorization of the neuron. You can now click on the Next Trial button to interact with another receptive field.

Your goal is to find and identify the receptive field of the neuron selected for the current trial. The receptive field types and their shapes are shown in the figure below. The simple and complex receptive fields have similar shapes, but the complex receptive field is actually, well, more complex than can be drawn. A complex receptive field can respond to light on either side of its receptive field, but it does not respond well to light on both sides of its receptive field. A simple receptive field is sensitive to light on only one, fixed side. For the simple neuron receptive field, the excitatory and inhibitory sides are randomly chosen.

The practice and experiment programs are nearly identical, except that the show receptive field button is always enabled in the practice version. This is to provide you with an opportunity to learn what types of stimuli are needed to drive the different cell types.

The receptive field will be randomly located on the canvas drawing surface. Your task is to find its location and draw an image that will get the neuron to respond strongly. You can then categorize it and move on to the next trial. Each receptive field is presented once, in random order.

This is a rather challenging experiment to finish. Once you are done you should have a pretty good idea of what a receptive field consists of, and the effects of excitation and inhibition. When you finish categorizing the last receptive field, a new window will appear that reports the time it took you to categorize each receptive field. Consider the effort neurophysiologists must exert to explore the receptive fields of real neurons.

Additional References

DeValois, R. L., Yund, E. W. & Hepler, N. (1982). The orientation and direction selectivity of cells in macaque visual cortex. *Vision Research, 22,* 531-544.

Hubel, D. H. & Wiesel, T. N. (1979). Brain mechanisms of vision. *Scientific American, 82,* 84-97.

Kuffler, S. W. (1953). Discharge patterns and functional organization of mammalian retina. *Journal of Neurophysiology, 16,* 37-68.

Basic Questions

1. Which receptive field took you the longest to categorize? Why might this be so?

2. What are cells with simple receptive fields set to detect in the visual environment?

3. What are cells with complex receptive fields set to detect in the visual environment?

Discussion Questions

1. Cells in the nervous system connect with each other in excitatory or inhibitory ways. How could sets of on-off concentric field cells connect together to build simple cells?

Sensory Memory – Metacontrast Masking

Masking refers to a class of phenomena where presentation of one stimulus (the mask) can impair performance on some task that requires judgment about another stimulus (the target). Visual masking plays two roles in cognitive science. First, masking is used to investigate properties of the visual system. By identifying the way in which the target and mask stimuli influence each other, vision scientists are able to deduce details about the underlying mechanisms involved in visual perception. Second, visual masking is used to indirectly restrict systems involved in information processing of visual stimuli. The logic of this type of approach is that the mask can halt further processing of the target and one can thereby explore the order and time course of many information processing systems. A special subset of this approach is based on evidence that persons with various types of cognitive disorders may respond differently than normal people under some masking conditions. Thus, masking has been proposed as a simple method for detecting some disorders and as a means of specifying the underlying mechanisms for those disorders.

Both the target and mask stimuli are usually very brief (often less than 200 milliseconds). Despite its short duration, if the target stimulus is presented by itself, it is clearly visible and it is easy for observers to perform whatever judgment is required of them. What is interesting is that the subsequent presentation of a mask stimulus, even a hundred milliseconds after the target has turned off, can make the observer's task of judging something about the target exceedingly difficult. When this effect was first noted by Stigler (1910), it forced the field of perceptual psychology to realize that processing of visual information took time and could be interrupted. Backward masking has been used to identify details of the perceptual and cognitive processes involved in building percepts and judgments.

Metacontrast masking is a specific type of masking where the target and mask have no overlapping contours and the mask follows the target in time. A surprising finding in studies of metacontrast masking is that when performance on some judgement about the target is plotted against the interstimulus interval (ISI) between the target and mask, the resulting curve is u-shaped. Performance is generally quite good when the mask immediately follows the target. Performance is also generally good for very long (greater than 200 milliseconds) ISIs. For ISI between 60 and 100 milliseconds, however, performance is often quite poor. Some observers report that they do not see the target at all.

The effect of the mask on the target sometimes gets stronger as the target and mask are separated in time, which is contrary to many simple models of visual perception. Investigations of the u-shaped metacontrast masking function is numerous and has identified a variety of characteristics about the visual system.

A window will fill the entire screen. Press the space bar key to start a trial. After pressing the space bar, a small fixation square will appear in the middle of the screen. Fixate this square. Half a second later one half dot (like a half moon) and three full dots will appear at the corners of an imaginary square around the fixation point. The half dot will be of random orientations. The stimuli will disappear after approximately 40 milliseconds. After a variable ISI, mask annuli will appear at each of the corners of the imaginary square. Your task is to report the orientation of the half-dot.

Make your selection by a key-press to indicate which side of the half-dot is missing. Press the i-key to indicate the top of the half dot is missing. Press the k-key to indicate the bottom of the half dot is missing. Press the j-key to indicate the left side of the dot is missing. Press the l-key to indicate the right side of the dot is missing. You can ignore all the other dots, only report on the orientation of the half dot.

With each key-press, a half dot will appear that corresponds to the selection you are making. You can change your choice by pressing another key. When you are satisfied with your choice, press the space bar key to start the next trial. Before the next trial begins, you will be given feedback on whether your choice was correct. You will notice an error when the shown half dot corresponding to your choice changes to the actual orientation of the half dot.

The experiment varies the ISI between offset of the target half dots and the masking annulus. There are seven ISIs, and 30 trials for each ISI. This makes for a total of 210 trials. That may sound like a lot, but each trial only takes a few seconds, so the entire experiment will not take very long. Moreover, you can take a break between trials if needed. You should try your best to correctly identify the missing side of the half dot. Do not, however, be concerned if you make a lot of mistakes. The expected result is that for some ISIs identification of the half dot will be very difficult. It can make the task somewhat frustrating, though.

At the end of the experiment a graph will appear that plots the percent of correct identifications of the half dot as a function of interstimulus interval (ISI) between the target and mask in milliseconds. You should find that the curve is u-shaped, with the bottom at an ISI somewhere between 40 and 120 milliseconds.

Additional References

Gilinsky, A. S. (1967). Orientation-specific effects of patterns of adapting light on visual acuity. *Journal of the Optical Society of America, 58,* 13-18.

Houlihan, K. & Sekuler, R. W. (1968). Contour interactions in visual masking. *Journal of Experimental Psychology, 77,* 281-285.

Werner, H. (1935). Studies in contour I: Qualitative analysis. *American Journal of Psychology, 47,* 40-64.

Basic Questions

1. Some people don't get a U-shaped curve in their data. Explain why this might happen.

2. The percent correct identification in your data is artificially high due to guessing. Explain what this means.

3. The existence of backward masking implies the operation of some sort of memory. Explain what this means.

Advanced Questions

A. From the plot of the mean percent correct identifications as a function of ISI find the ISI for which performance is worst. Is it where predicted?

B. Compare the graph of your own data with the graph of the group data in (A). Which one shows a smoother relationship?

Discussion Questions

1. Do you think that backward masking operates in the real world to make it hard to see? Explain your answer.
2. Perceiving the visual world involves active processing of incoming stimuli. What types of processes might the mask be interfering with?

Sensory Memory – Modality Effect

People often have to recall a series of items in order, such as when recalling a phone number. When the list of items is heard (as opposed to read silently), people usually are very good at remembering the final list item. This advantage in recalling just the last one or two items when the list is heard is called the modality effect.

Modality effects can be seen with presentation modalities other than auditory (hearing). Lists that are lip-read or silently mouthed also produce an advantage for the last one or two items compared to silent visual presentation.

These effects had an enormous influence on the development of sensory memory. This memory system is supposed to store raw, unanalyzed sensory input. It can be thought of as a back-up system: if the information in this store is useful, recall can be enhanced.

The best explanation is that auditory presentation leads to an additional type of information compared to visual (Neath & Surprenant, 2003). When trying to recall the last item in the list, you are more likely to be successful if you also have some information about how the list sounds.

Before the demonstration begins, make sure the volume on your computer/speakers is set at a comfortable level. If you are running this lab in a public space, please use headphones so that you do not disturb other people.

Start a trial by pressing the *Next Trial* button. You will either hear the digits 1-9 spoken in random order, or you will see them displayed on the left part of the screen in random order. After the entire list has been presented, the response buttons will become active. Your task is to click on the buttons *in the same order* that the digits were presented. After you have finished clicking on all the buttons to recreate the list, click on *Next Trial* to start the next sequence.

Being correct means that you click on the buttons in the same order the items appeared in the sequence. There is no way to correct mistakes in button presses, so be careful in your selections.

There are 30 trials, 15 visual and 15 auditory trials randomly intermixed.

When the experiment finishes, a new window will appear that gives the proportion of items you recalled at each list position in the visual condition and in the auditory condition. You should do very well recalling the first item in both conditions. However, you should be much more accurate in recalling the last item when it was heard compared to when it was seen.

Basic Questions

1. Of the eight letters presented in the experiment, which letters had the lowest rate of recall? Which had the best rate of recall?

2. For the letter in the last position of the list to be recalled, which mode of list presentation had the higher rate of percentage recalled?

3. If you were making out your appointments for the day that you have to remember, why would it make more sense to say them out loud to yourself after writing them out, rather than just righting them down in your daily planner.

4. You are trying to decide whether or not to buy a CD that accompanies one of your textbooks. The CD is expensive, but it has a number of interactive activities and an auditory glossary. You are struggling in this class and you are concerned about your grades. If money is not an issue, should you purchase the CD or not?

5. You are following along with your favorite cooking show and trying to make fudge cake. They don't have time to go through the icing so they flash the ingredients on the screen during a break. Your icing doesn't taste right and you think that you forgot an item. If the recipe was visually presented on the screen, would it make sense that you forgot the last item in the recipe?

Advanced Questions

A. You have been hired to design a fresh new commercial for your University. Your goal is to have people remember the name of the University after the commercial is over. How could you use the modality effect to your advantage in making your commercial?

B. You are responsible for advertising the last class bash for your organization and you want to make it the largest that it has ever been. You can either advertise in the campus newspaper or on the campus radio station. You choose to advertise with the radio station because the listening audience is greater. How can you use the modality effect to help design your catchy announcement so people remember to come to the party? Remember the mode of presentation.

Discussion Questions

1. Discuss how the modality effect is related to the idea of *Cognitive load*. According to this idea, learning will be impaired if the material causes a cognitive overload. Since the working memory is very limited, how would varying the modality reduce the cognitive load?

2. How could the results of this lab help you with improve your performance on tests as well as your overall academic performance?

Sensory Memory – Partial Report

In the early beginnings of psychology, researchers were interested in something called the "perceptual span." This quest was to determine how much information could be gathered in a single percept. For example, when you read text, how many letters can you interpret in a single glance? Or, how many coins can you distinguish if you briefly glance at them? The goal was to identify the limits of perceptual abilities. A variety of ingenious studies seemed to draw similar conclusions that people could accurately report about 4.5 items from a brief percept. This fact was built into many theories of cognition until a set of experiments by George Sperling (1960) proved it wrong.

Sperling suggested that the 4.5 item limit was imposed not by the capabilities of the perceptual system, but by observers' abilities to recall items that had been seen. To test this possibility he designed a partial report experiment. This laboratory allows you to participate in a version of this experiment.

In Sperling's original experiment, the observer saw a three by three matrix of random letters on each trial. The letters were flashed for a very short period of time (50 milliseconds). After the letter matrix turned off, one of three tones sounded, and the observer reported the letters from the row associated with the tone. If the tone was presented directly after offset of the letters, Sperling found that observers were nearly 100% accurate in reporting letters from the indicated row.

This result destroys theories that hypothesized that percepts hold only 4—5 items. Because the tone was sounded after the letters disappeared, observers must be focusing on the appropriate row as it is stored in some type of sensory store of perceptual information. Moreover, since perfect performance is found regardless of which row is indicated, the sensory store must contain a nearly perfect representation of the total visual percept. Thus, perceptual span was not 4.5 items, but essentially every item in the visual field.

What determined perceptual span in the earlier experiments was not limits of the perceptual system, but the time needed to report the seen items. The duration of information in sensory store is very brief (a few hundred milliseconds), so as observers report what they see, items in sensory store fade away. By the time observers report on 4 or 5 items, the sensory store information is gone and recall is finished.

Sperling also found a way to measure the duration of information in sensory store. When he increased the time between the offset of the letter matrix and the onset of the tone cue, he found that recall of letters became worse. If the tone was delayed by a full second, recall was comparable to the 4.5 items found in other experiments.

When these experimental results were reported in 1960 they revolutionized both our understanding of perception and memory and the experimental methods with which cognitive psychology was studied. There have subsequently been thousands of studies on the sensory (also called iconic) store and it is a part of many theories of cognition.

After clicking on the start button, a window will fill the entire screen. Press the space bar to start a trial; the screen will go dark and a small fixation square will appear in the middle of the screen. Fixate this square. It will disappear after one and a half seconds. Half a second letter a three by three matrix of letters will be flashed for 150 milliseconds. Some time after the offset of the letter matrix, an arrow (>) will indicate which row you are to report. Type the letters from the indicated row. Guess if you do not know what the letters were. You can make up to three guesses for every trial.

When you are ready, press the space bar for the next trial. There are a total of 60 trials, with the same basic task in every one. Simply report the letters that flashed from the indicated row. As you go through the experiment, keep your eyes steady on the fixation mark, then do not move them until after the matrix disappears. There is no method for discarding a trial in this experiment, so try to make certain you are ready as you start a trial.

At the end of the experiment a graph will appear that plots the percentage of letters correctly reported as a function of the delay between letter matrix offset and arrow indicator onset (in milliseconds). As the delay increases from 20 to 1000 milliseconds, you should find that the percentage correct drops.

The number of letters in your sensory store would be the total number of letters in the matrix (9) multiplied by the proportion (percentage divided by 100) of items you reported. For the 1000 millisecond (one second) delay, you may find that your proportion multiplied by 9 is about 4.5 items.

Additional References

Averbach, E. & Coriell, A. S. (1961). Short-term memory in vision. *Bell System Technical Journal, 40,* 309-328.

Coltheart, M. (1980). Iconic memory and visual persistence. *Perception and Psychophysics, 27,* 183-228.

Massaro, D. W. & Loftus, G. R. (1996). Sensory and perceptual store. In E. L. Bjork & R. A. Bjork (Eds.), *Memory.* San Diego, CA: Academic Press.

Mewhort, D. J. K. & Leppman, K. P. (1985). Information persistence: Testing spatial and identity information with a voice probe. *Psychological Research, 47,* 51-58.

Sperling, G. (1963). A model for visual memory tasks. *Human Factors, 5,* 19-31.

Basic Questions

1. Do your results confirm the general findings of the partial report?

2. You probably tried very hard in this demonstration to report all the letters you possibly could at even the longest delays. Do you think that there might be a way to make the sensory store last longer in order to improve your performance at longer delays?

3. Why do you think that we have a sensory store? What could it be used for when reading text?

Advanced Questions

A. Use the group plot of the mean percentage of letters correctly reported as a function of cue delay to find the duration of the icon.

Discussion Questions

1. Perceiving the visual world involves processing incoming stimulation. How does iconic memory fit into this idea?

2. Do you think the icon is particularly useful in ordinary day-to-day visual perception?

3. Explain the logic behind saying that the duration of the icon is that indicator arrow delay at which the partial report results equal the full repot results.

Sensory Memory – Suffix Effect

People often have to recall a series of items in order, such as when recalling a phone number. When the list of items is heard (as opposed to read silently), people usually are very good at remembering the final list item. However, if the list is followed by an irrelevant item (the suffix), recall of the final item is substantially impaired.

The suffix has to be perceived as speech in order for it to have a large effect. If the suffix is a pure tone, there is no impairment. Although the suffix has to be speech, it does not have to be a word. In general, the suffix will have a larger effect the more acoustically similar it is to the list items.

One reason that the suffix effect has attracted a lot of attention is that recall is impaired even when the suffix is expected and even when the suffix is the same item (usually the digit 0) on every trial.

The best explanation is that when the suffix is perceptually grouped with the list items, it functionally increases the list length. So, rather than trying to recall a 9 item list, you are in effect recalling a 10 item list (Neath, 1998).

Start a trial by pressing the Next Trial button. You will hear the digits 1-8 spoken in random order. On half the trials, you will here a tone after the final item; on the remaining trials, you will hear the digit 0. After the tone or speech suffix has been presented, the response buttons will become active. Your task is to click on the buttons in the same order that the letters were presented. After you have finished clicking on all the buttons to recreate the list, click on Next Trial to start the next sequence.

Being correct means that you click on the buttons in the same order the items appeared in the sequence. There is no way to correct mistakes in button presses, so be careful in your selections.

There are 30 trials, 15 suffix and 15 tone trials randomly intermixed.

When the experiment finishes, a new window will appear that gives the proportion of items you recalled at each list position in the speech suffix condition and in the tone suffix condition. You should do very well recalling the last item when it was followed by a tone, but you should do very poorly when the item was followed by a speech suffix.

Additional References

Pilotti, M., Beyer, T. & Yasunami, M. (2002). Top-down processing and the suffix effect in young and older adults. *Memory & Cognition, 30* (1).

Surprenant, A. M., LeCompte, D. C., & Neath, I. (2000). Manipulations of irrelevant information: Suffix effects with articulatory suppression and irrelevant speech. *Quarterly Journal of Experimental Psychology, 53A*, 325-348.

Basic Questions

1. If the "0" on the end of the list of words was predictable, meaning it happened ever time, do you think it would it still affect your memory? Why or why not?

2. If we were talking about memory resources, how does the added suffix at the end of list affect your memory for the list of words? How did the tone affect your memory for the list?

3. You are talking to your friend on his CB radio about a great party that he knows about. He tells you to call him on his new cell phone if you need a ride because you are not sure where it is and proceeds to quickly give you his number – 6-4-7-5-3-6-5. As you being to repeat the number to yourself, you hear your friend on the other end say "10-4 good buddy" and the line goes dead. How did he mess up your ability to remember his phone number?

4. Somehow you find yourself being dragged to a charity Bingo game hosted by your sorority. Half way through a game you have to excuse yourself to make an important phone call. When you return to the table, your friends tell you that they missed blocking out the called numbers on your cards but they proceed to quickly recite the numbers that were called while you were gone – 3-52-35-7-41-23-15 and 21. As you reach for your dabber, the Bingo caller yells "Under the B-10" and you forget all of the numbers that you were repeating to yourself. Would this have happened if the number 10 was visually displayed while a bell sounded to direct player's attention towards a board that had all the called numbers lit up on it?

5. It is Thanksgiving and you are having dinner with your new boyfriend's family, his very large family. Before sitting down at a huge dinner table, he begins introducing you to his family. After giving you about 10 names to remember, his nephew brings up this cute puppy and tells you his name is "Roger". When you sit down to eat, you look out at the strange faces and you can only remember the first three and then you draw a blank. How did "Roger" affect your memory?

Advanced Questions

A. There are two main ideas about how we filter information from our environments. According to one theory, we filter late, meaning we take in all information and then decide if we need to use it for our response. The other idea is that we filter early or we take in only a certain amount of information and block the rest. Decide which of these two competing theories best explain the results of this lab and explain why?

B. As explained by serial position curve, memory for the beginning (primacy effect) and the end of a list (recency effect) seem to be better when compared to the information in the middle. What would the added suffix do for each of this phenomenon in terms of memory recall?

C. If visually presented stimuli did not have a similar interference effect on memory recall than verbally presented material, what could be said about the differences between the memory stores for each of the methods of presentation (verbal and visual)?

Discussion Questions

1. If your professor told you that the Suffix Effect was stronger in verbally presented material than in visually presented information, what suggestions would you have for teachers when presenting class materials?

2. We know that we have limited resources when it comes to such cognitive activities like memory. Discuss possible tricks that you use to improve your memory for important information?

Short-Term Memory – Brown-Peterson

In the 1940's memory loss was widely considered to be the result of new information interfering with previously learned information. In the late 1950's two groups of researchers (one named Brown and a husband and wife team named Peterson) published data that forced a new interpretation of human memory.

In the memory task, the participant viewed a trigram of consonants (e.g., GKT, WCH,...) and then performed a number of algebraic computations (e.g., counting backwards by 3's) for less than 20 seconds. The data showed that recall of the trigram was less likely as the participant worked on the algebraic computations for longer durations.

Solving math problems seems to be very different from recalling consonant trigrams, so it was unlikely that there was any interference to disturb the memory of the trigram. The conclusion was that there exists a short-term memory (STM) system that holds information for several seconds. Without an active effort by the participant, information in STM fades away (but see Keppel & Underwood, 1962, for an alternate explanation). Performing the distracter task prevented the participant from actively rehearsing the trigram. STM is now a fundamental part of most theories of cognitive psychology.

A few seconds after clicking on the start button, a window will. The left side contains a blank screen and two buttons bellow. The right side of the screen contains a set of buttons. Start the experiment by clicking on the Next Trial button.

On the left screen a trigram of letters will appear for two seconds. You will then be prompted to click on the button (below) that has an even number as its label. The duration of time spent identifying which button has an even label will vary from one to twenty-one seconds. After correct completion of the identification task you will be prompted to recall the consonant trigram. From the buttons on the right, select the consonants, in the correct order, that appeared before the identification task. After you have entered your guess, and are ready for the next trial, click on Next Trial button again.

For the trial to count, you must have correctly identified the even-labeled buttons. If your identification is incorrect, the trial will be repeated later in the experiment. Thus, to finish the experiment you must apply yourself to the identification task. There are a total of 30 trials that must be run to finish the experiment.

At the end of the experiment a graph will appear that plots the percentage of correctly recalled trigrams as a function of the duration of the distracter task (digit classification). For this calculation, a recall is correct only if it includes all the trigram letters in their correct order. You should find that the percentage correct decreases as distracter duration increases.

Additional References

Brown, J. (1958). Some tests of the decay theory of immediate memory. *Quarterly Journal of Experimental Psychology, 10,* 12-21.

Gardiner, J. M., Craik, F. I. M. & Birtwistle, J. (1972). Retrieval cues and release from proactive inhibition. *Journal of Verbal Learning and Verbal Behavior, 11,* 778-783.

Keppel, G. & Underwood, B. J. (1962). Proactive inhibition in short-term retention of single items. *Journal of Verbal Learning and Verbal Behavior, 1,* 153-161.

Peterson, L. R. & Peterson, M. J. (1959). Short-term retention of individual items. *Journal of Experimental Psychology, 58,* 193-198.

Turvey, M. T., Brick, P. & Osborn, J. (1970). Proactive interference in short-term memory as a function of prior-item retention interval. *Quarterly Journal of Experimental Psychology, 22,* 142-147.

Basic Questions

1. What does "actively rehearsing the trigram" mean? (Hint: the distractor task *prevents* active rehearsal.)

2. Suppose we used trigrams like "JOE" or "CAT" or "WXY" or "RIT" rather than the type used in the demonstration. Describe what the relationship between percent correct recall and number of seconds of distracter task might be compared to the one that Brown and Peterson obtained.

3. The way that the contents of short term memory are assessed seems rather restricted in this demonstration. Suggest two ways to modify that assessment so that performance might improve.

Advanced Questions

A. From the plot of the group mean percent correctly recalled trigrams as a function of distractor task interval decide the Brown-Peterson findings were confirmed.

Discussion Questions

1. Put together a good argument for the operation of decay during forgetting from short term memory.

2. Put together a good argument for the operation of interference during forgetting from short term memory.

3. Based on what you know about the Brown-Peterson task and related experiments, suggest some ways to reduce forgetting from short term memory.

Short-Term Memory – Irrelevant Speech Effect

When people are asked to recall a list of items, their performance is usually worse when presentation of the list is accompanied by irrelevant speech. The speech does not need to be in a language that the subject knows, and doesn't even have to be real speech. Nonsense speech (such as "ba da ga") works just as well. One reason that this phenomenon, known as the irrelevant speech effect, has attracted a lot of attention is because it seems strange that auditory information (the irrelevant speech stimuli) would interfere with visual information (the items you are trying to remember).

Although there is still no generally agreed upon explanation for this effect, there are at least three different explanations (Neath, 2000). One theory attributes the disruption to interference in working memory. The visual items are translated into a phonological code that is stored in the same part of memory (the phonological store) as the irrelevant speech. Another attributes the effect to a disruption of order information. You remember the items, but it is information about the order that is lost. A third attributes the effect to a combination of two factors, an attentional component and an interference component.

Start a trial by pressing the Next Trial button. On the left of the window will appear a sequence of letters, with each letter presented for one second. After the full sequence has been presented, the buttons on the right will show labels for the letters, including those just shown. Your task is to click on the buttons just shown in the same order that the letters were presented. After you have finished clicking on all the buttons to recreate the list, click on Next Trial to start the next sequence.

The experiment includes two types of trials: Some trials are presented with irrelevant speech (a passage from Franz Kafka in German) and some are presented with no irrelevant speech. The order of the conditions is random.

Being correct means that you both recall all the items in the sequence and click on the buttons in the same order the items appeared in the sequence. Any mistake (recalling too many items, recalling too few items, or recalling items in the wrong order) counts as Incorrect. There is no way to correct mistakes in button presses, so be careful in your selections.

When the experiment finishes, a new window will appear that gives the proportion of items you recalled in the quiet condition and the proportion of items you recalled in the irrelevant speech condition. You should do worse when there is irrelevant speech.

Additional References

Ellermeier, W. & Hellbrück, J. (1998). Is level irrelevant in "irrelevant speech"? Effects of loudness, signal-to-noise ratio and binaural unmasking. *Journal of Experimental Psychology: Human Perception and Performance, 24*, 1406-1414.

Macken, W.J., Mosdell, N., & Jones, D.M. (1999). Explaining the irrelevant sound effect: Temporal distinctiveness or changing state? *Journal of Experimental Psychology: Learning, Memory and Cognition, 25,* 810-814.

Basic Questions

1. How could you change the methodology of this lab to study what specific kind of stimuli produce greater memory interference effects, irrelevant noise or irrelevant speech?

2. If you found that irrelevant speech interfered with your memory for visually presented material over irrelevant noise, what might this suggest to you about the kind of background music you could listen to while studying?

3. You are trying to study in the library but there are people beside you whispering and talking. Could this situation be affecting your studying performance? Why or why not?

4. You are trying to watch an intense psychological thriller on television and you need to follow the characters actions very closely to understand what is going on. Your roommate, however, is walking around the apartment muttering into his cell phone. How is he affecting your ability to follow the characters in the movie?

5. If you were studying for your final exam in Biology and you haven't been doing well in the term so you need an "A" to pass this course, how could this lab help to structure your studying environment?

Advanced Questions

A. One theory that is used to explain the results of this lab is that there may be a disruption of the order of the to-be-remembered information. How could you add or re-examine the dependent measures of this lab so that you could address this theory?

B. You are trying to find your way to a friend's house for a party. You've been there once before but that was a long time ago. As you find yourself getting lost and driving in circles, you immediately turn your music down. After doing this lab, explain why this might make sense.

C. You work in a call center for an international company on the weekends for extra money. Everyone sits in a large warehouse behind small cubicles while dealing with customers on the phone. What kind of problems could you have in this kind of work environment that takes the irrelevant speech effect into consideration?

Discussion Questions

1. Discuss others areas in society, besides school, where you might find examples of the irrelevant speech effect. Be specific about the place and possible problems this effect might cause

2. From a methodological standpoint, there may be other factors that affect the degree of memory loss in the irrelevant speech effect. Some factors may include things like loudness of speech (reference provided), gender of speech, different languages or the number of different stimuli presented (more than one speech at the same time). Hypothesize how these and other factors you can think of may influence the overall effect. You can refer to the specific parts of the working memory; phonological loop; visuospatial pad and the executive control or other knowledge you have about memory, when formulating your hypotheses.

Short-Term Memory – Memory Span

Many theories of cognition propose that there is a short-term or working memory system that is able to hold a limited amount of information for a short period of time. The memory span experiment is one measure of working memory capacity. In this experiment participants are given a list of items and asked to recall the list. The list length is varied to see at what list length participants will make few errors. That list length is the memory span for that subject on that task. Individuals with larger memory spans can better keep in mind different stimuli, and this seems to give them an advantage for a wide variety of cognitive tasks. Memory span has been linked to performance on intelligence tests, standardized tests, reading skills, problem solving and a variety of other cognitive tasks.

The very existence of short-term memory is largely based on memory span types of experiments, as it was noted that memory span was approximately seven (plus or minus two) for a wide variety of stimuli. This suggested a simple storage system that held approximately seven items. Later studies demonstrated that memory span could be systematically influenced by a variety of stimulus characteristics. For example, when the stimuli are letters that sound alike (e.g., d, b, p, t) memory span is shorter. Likewise, memory span is shorter for lists of long words (e.g., encyclopedia, refrigerator) than for lists of short words (e.g., book, stove). These findings have suggested that verbal processes control the capacity of short-term memory. This experiment allows you to measure your memory span for a variety of stimulus types.

Start a trial by pressing the Next Trial button. On the left of the window will appear a sequence of items, with each item presented for one second. After the full sequence has been presented, the buttons on the right will show labels for item names, including those just shown. Your task is to click on the buttons just shown in the same order that the items were presented. After you have finished clicking on all the buttons to recreate the list, click on Next Trial to start the next sequence.

The experiment includes five types of stimuli: Numbers, Letters that sound different, Letters that sound the same, Short words, and Long words. In each case your task is simply to report the items you saw, in the order they were presented. Each stimulus type will be presented five times, with varying list lengths.

List length is varied, for each type of stimuli, to find the longest list for which you can correctly recreate the sequence. Being correct means that you both recall all the items in the sequence and click on the buttons in the same order the items appeared in the sequence. Any mistake (recalling too many items, recalling too few items, or recalling items in the wrong order) counts as Incorrect. There is no way to correct mistakes in button presses, so be careful in your selections. After clicking on Next Trial, you will be given feedback on your response to the previous sequence (Correct/Incorrect) before the next sequence is presented.

If you are correct for a given sequence, then the next sequence for that stimulus type will be one item longer. If you are incorrect, the next sequence for that stimulus type will be one item shorter. In this way, the length of the sequence converges on the longest list length that you can reliably report back.

When the experiment finishes, a new window will appear that gives the length of the last sequence for each stimulus type. This is an estimate of your memory span.

The literature on memory span suggests that the memory span for Numbers, Letters that sound different, and Short words should be around seven items. Memory span for Letters that sound the same and Long words should be shorter. There are five trials for each stimulus type. The maximum memory span measurable with this experiment is ten, so if you were correct on the last trial for a stimulus type and your list length was ten, your memory span may actually be greater. This would indicate that you have an excellent short-term memory.

Additional References

Baddeley, A. D. & Logie, R. H. (1999). Working memory: The multiple-component model. In A. Miyake & P. Shah (Eds.), *Models of working memory: Mechanisms of active maintenance and executive control* (pp. 28-61). New York, NY, USA: Cambridge University Press.

Miller, G. A. (1956). The magical number seven plus or minus two: Some limits on our capacity for processing information. *Psychological Review, 63,* 81-97.

Page, M. P. A. & Norris, D. (1998). The primacy model: a new model of immediate serial recall. *Psychological Review, 105*, 761-781.

If you want a model, choose:
Brown, G. D. A. & Hulme, C. (1995). Modeling item length effects in memory span: No rehearsal needed? *Journal of Memory and Language, 34*, 594-621.

If you want to demonstrate the generality of the effect, choose:
Schweickert, R. & Boruff, B. (1986). Short-term memory capacity: Magic number or magic spell? *Journal of Experimental Psychology: Learning, Memory and Cognition, 12*, 419-425.

For an alternate interpretation, choose:
Nairne, J. S. & Neath, I. (2001). Long-term memory span. *Behavioral and Brain Sciences, 24*, 134-135.

Basic Questions

1. Describe three ways this task could be made easier so that your memory span became longer.

2. Explain how memory span might be based on "verbal processes". (Hint: for sound-alikes or for longer words, the memory span goes down.)

3. Why do you think that memory span might be related to reading and problem solving?

Advanced Questions

A. Using the group mean length of the last sequence for each stimulus type, decide if the data confirms the effect of stimulus type on memory span discussed in the experiment.

Discussion Questions

1. Suggest some ways to increase memory span.

2. Memory span capacity limits affect the work that working memory does. Discuss some of the effects on working memory.

3. Discuss why there is so much variability in memory span.

Short-Term Memory – Position Error

Many tasks require people to remember not only a set of items but also the order of the items. For example, a telephone number is meaningful only if the items are recalled in the correct order. When people do not recall an item in its correct order, the errors they make are systematic.

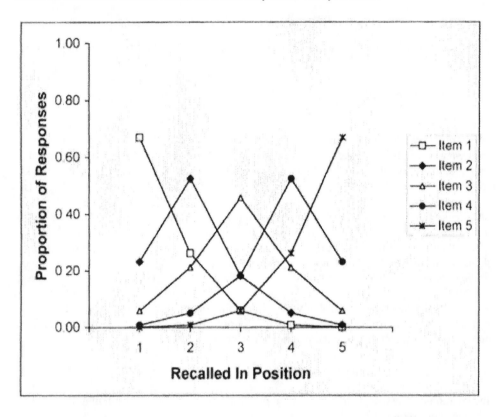

The graph above shows what these systematic errors would look like when people try to recall a five-item list in order. Most of the time, the items are recalled in the correct position. So, the line marked "Item 1" has its largest value at position 1; the line marked "Item 2" has its largest value at position 2; and so on. When an order error is made, the graph shows that the item is most likely to be recalled either 1 position too soon or 1 position too late. So, when Item 3 is not recalled in position 3, it is most likely to be recalled in position 2 or position 4.

Results like these have important implications for theories of memory. If all you look at is percent correct, then you might think that forgetting means that the information is lost from the memory system. However, you are still remembering something about the item: you usually recall the item in a position adjacent to the correct position.

Start a trial by clicking on the Next Trial button. On the left of the window will appear a sequence of 7 letters, with each letter presented for one second. After the full sequence has been presented, the buttons on the right will show labels for items just shown. Your task is to click on the buttons in the same order that the letters were presented. If you think the first letter was M, click on the button labeled M first. If you think the sixth letter was F, click on the button labeled F sixth.

After you have finished clicking on all the buttons to recreate the list, click on Next Trial to start the next sequence. There are 20 trials.

When the experiment finishes, a new window will appear that tells you the proportion of times you recalled each item in each position. You should find that your data look similar to the data shown in the graph: You should be most likely to recall an item in its original serial position, but when you made an error, the item should be most likely to be in an adjacent position.

Basic Questions

1. When trying to recall the seven letters in order, which letter position should have shown the lowest rate of correct responses?

2. If the series of letters to be recalled were, MXFGKLC, which letter(s) would have the greatest probability of mistaking in the letter K's position?

3. You are trying to remember the phone number, (705) 647-5893, but you do not have a pen to write it down. When you try to dial it, you make a mistake and dial, (705) 647-8593. Why does this misdial seem more possible than mixing up the 3 and the 8? What does this say about the errors that we make, are they random or systematic?

4. You excitedly check your grade online to see how well your extensive studying worked for your cognitive exam. Your excitement fades fast when you see a failing grade for that test and you immediately find your professor. After checking, she notices that she has mixed up your grade with another students when copying them to the online grade sheets. After doing this lab, explain how she could have mixed up the grades?

5. You are trying out for the cheerleader squad at your school, but you are having trouble with the routine. The cheer goes; step, turn, kick, touch, leap, jump, splits, but you are leaping then touching. How can your error be explained through the position error gradient?

Advanced Questions

A. What does the position error experiment tell us about our short- term memory system that the serial position effect does not expand on?

B. Before doing this lab, you have always wondered why the Biology Lab Teaching Assistant is always calling you David, when your name is Sean. Why did this experiment explain this error to you?

Discussion Questions

1. Discuss why it would be important to know what specific kinds of errors we make in terms of retrieving or recalling information?

2. Discuss how the results from this lab could help you improve your memory for lists of items that have to be recalled in a specific order. Think in terms of attention.

Short-Term Memory – Operation Span

Recent conceptions of memory have suggested that memory consists of a flexible workspace that not only stores information but also plays an active role in processing and manipulating information. This active process, however, seems to have a limited amount of resources to work with. One question that has been posed is whether the capacity is specific to verbal tasks or whether there is a general pool of resources that is used in every working memory task. Most previous researchers have used only verbal materials in measuring working memory capacity.

To determine whether there is a general capacity for all working memory tasks Turner and Engle (1989) developed a task called "operation-word-span" (OSPAN). In this task subjects are asked to read and verify a simple math problem (such as (4/2)-1=1) and then read a word after the operation (such as SNOW). After a series of problems and words had been presented, the subjects recall the words that followed each operation. The number of operation-word strings in a sequence is increased and decreased to measure the subject's operation span. Operation span measures predict verbal abilities and reading comprehension even though the subjects are solving mathematical problems. Engle and his colleagues have argued that this implicates a general pool of resources that is used in every type of working memory situation.

This demonstration allows you to measure your operation span using the procedure of Conway & Engle (1996).

Start a trial by pressing the Next Trial button. You will see a math problem of the form:

Is $10/2 + 2 = 7$?

Read the math problem out loud and then decide whether the given answer is correct or incorrect. If the problem is correct, click once on the yes button; if the problem is incorrect, click once on the no button.

You will then see a word. Read the word out loud. You will then see another math problem.

At some point, you will be asked to recall all the words from the series. Simply click on the buttons that are labeled with words you have just seen in the order in which you saw the words.

Your operation span score is valid only if you were more than 85% accurate in evaluating the math problems.

If you were more than 85% accurate in evaluating the math problems, you will see your operation span score at the end of the demonstration. This score is the sum of the sequence lengths you recalled correctly. Thus, if you recalled the list of 2 words correctly, you would add 2 to your operation span score. If you recalled the list of 6 items correctly, you would add 6 to your operation span.

The first three trials were all of length 2, and were considered practice trials. Performance on these trials does not affect your accuracy score or you operation span score.

The literature on working memory capacity suggests that operation span correlates well with performance on other tasks, including ones involving memory and attention.

Additional References

Conway, A. & Engle, R. (1996). Individual differences in working memory capacity: More evidence for a general capacity theory. *Memory 4*, 577-590.

Hitch, G., Towse, J. & Una Hutton, U. (2001). What limits children's working memory span? Theoretical accounts and applications for scholastic development. *Journal of Experimental Psychology: General, 130*, 184-198.

Basic Questions

1. Why do you think that your Operation Span would only be valid if it were 85% or higher on the math problems?

2. Why did the math problems and the words have to be read out loud instead of being done silently?

3. You are talking to some fellow classmates at a party in your residence. The friend you are talking to points to another group of people looking at you and laughing and you are curious what they are laughing about. When you go over to the group of people you see your best friend in the middle and she says that she was telling that group about a funny story that involved you but you didn't turn around when she yelled your name. What can be inferred about your ability to block out distractions and your Operation Span?

4. You are amazed by your boyfriend who can sit in front of the television set during Superbowl and never hear a word you have said for 2 hours, while you can complete conversations on the telephone using both lines, read the newspaper, do your nails, bake cookies and think about a math problem from class that day. In terms of controlling attention, how do the two of you compare?

5. Your father is teaching you to drive but you are having trouble remembering everything that you have to do to keep safe while on the road. Your father suggests that you say everything that you are doing out loud, so it will help you focus as you are performing the task. How is that comparable to this lab?

Advanced Questions

A.- Although the Operation Span lab is found under the subcategory of memory, how is attention related to this phenomenon?

B. After doing this lab you discover that you have a relatively high OSPAN compared to your classmates. How might this affect your studying habits?

C. How could the three specific areas of working memory (phonological loop, visuospatial sketchpad and the executive control system) work together to perform this lab?

Discussion Questions

1. People with higher Operation Spans are said to be better at controlling their attention and are less affected by distractions. Discuss some situations where this may not be a good thing?

2. The concept of one's Operation Span has been correlated to reading ability and verbal comprehension. Why does this seem like a logical relationship?

Short-Term Memory – Sternberg Search

Many researchers of memory believe that there exists a short-term memory (STM) system that holds information for a few seconds. If the information in STM is not transferred to long term memory (LTM) for more permanent storage, it vanishes. As evidence on the existence of STM grew, researchers started to explore its properties. In a series of articles starting in 1966 Saul Sternberg developed an experimental approach to explore how information was retrieved from STM.

The basic approach is simple. Subjects were shown a short (one to six items) list of numbers and asked to memorize them. After putting them to memory, a probe number was shown. The probe number was either one of the numbers in the list or a new number. The subject was to respond as quickly as possible whether the probe number was in the list or not. The reaction time of the subject should reflect the time spent searching STM to determine whether the probe number is part of the list. By varying the number of items in the list Sternberg hypothesized that he could test several theories of STM search.

For example, some types of neural network theories of memory suggest that every item in memory can be accessed simultaneously due to the parallel nature of search in these networks. If such a search took place in STM, one would expect the reaction times not to vary as number of items (memory set size) increased.

On the other hand, if memory search required consideration of each item in succession, the reaction times should increase with memory set size because the subject will, on average, have to search through more items. Sternberg's data was consistent with the successive (or serial) search.

Sternberg found two additional properties that were interesting. First, reaction times grew linearly with increases in memory set size. For each additional item in the memory set, subjects took (on average) additional 38 milliseconds to make their response. Thus, it seems the probe item is compared one-by-one with each item in STM, and each comparison takes approximately 38 milliseconds.

Second, when he compared reaction times for probe "Present" and "Absent" trials (probe item was in the memory set or not, respectively), Sternberg found no differences in reaction times. This finding is notable because an "Absent" response can only be made after all items in STM have been searched and found to not match the probe item. At first glance it might seem that a "Present" trial could terminate as soon as the probe item is matched with the appropriate item in STM. As a result, with a self-terminating search, one would expect "Present" trials to be faster, but the data contradict this hypothesis.

The counterintuitive finding from Sternberg's study is that search of STM is always exhaustive. That is, the cognitive processes responsible for searching STM for a particular item search through all items in STM before reporting whether the probe item is in memory or not.

Sternberg's study and his analysis of the data had a major influence on models of memory and cognitive psychology in general. While more recent modeling approaches have shown that the implications of the data on theories of memory search are not as straightforward as once believed, the experimental approach and theorizing is classic. (For a recent review of the field see Van Zandt and Townsend (1993).) This experiment allows you to participate in a variation of the Sternberg memory search task.

Start a trial by pressing the space bar. A fixation point will appear in the middle of the screen. After a second, a memory set consisting of 1, 3, or 5 numbers will appear on the screen for 1.2, 3.6, or 6 seconds, respectively. Study the numbers and commit them to memory. The memory set will disappear and then 1 to 3 seconds later a probe item will appear. Your task is to determine whether the probe item was in the list of just presented numbers. Respond as quickly as possible by pressing the / key (for "Present") or z key (for "Absent"). You will receive feedback on whether you were correct. When you are ready for the next trial press the space bar again.

There is a minimum of 60 trials in the experimental session. For each "Present" and "Absent" condition 10 trials are presented for each memory set size. If you make a mistake (e.g., say the item was present when it was not), the trial will be repeated (with different numbers) later in the experiment. In this way, only reaction times where you were correct are used. If you find you are often making mistakes, you should try slowing down on your responses and/or try harder.

If you are distracted during a trial (e.g., you sneezed, attention drifted, you "zoned out", ...) press the t key instead of z or /. This will discard the trial. Press the space bar to start the next trial. The discarded trial will be rerun later in the experiment.

When you finish the experiment, a window will appear that plots reaction time as a function of memory set size, with separate curves for "Present" and "Absent" trials. You should find that both curves increase with set size, and that the curves are nearly straight lines. Sternberg found that the "Present" and "Absent" curves were nearly superimposed, but you may not find that to be true (Sternberg's subjects had more practice and were paid to be highly motivated). Your data would agree with Sternberg's general findings if your curves were parallel. If your curves diverge as set size increases, your data is not consistent with Sternberg's general findings.

Additional References

DeRosa, D. V. & Tkacz, D. (1976). Memory scanning on organized visual material. *Journal of Experimental Psychology: Human Learning and Memory, 2,* 688-694.

Sternberg, S. (1966). High-speed scanning in human memory. *Science, 153,* 652-654.

Sternberg, S. (1967). Two operations in character recognition: Some evidence from reaction time measurements. *Perception & Psychophysics, 2,* 45-53.

Sternberg, S. (1969). Memory-scanning: Mental processes revealed by reaction time experiments. *American Scientist, 57,* 421-457.

Basic Questions

1. If the search process were terminating rather than exhaustive, how would that affect the "absent" line on the graph?

2. If the search were done in parallel how would that affect the "present" line on the graph?

3. Most people *don't* have the experience of examining the memory set one item at a time for the probe until the whole set has been examined in their minds. So if Sternberg is right about exhaustive serial search taking place *and* we aren't aware of it taking place, what conclusion should we draw about how the mind *really* works and the way it *seems* to work when we use it?

Advanced Questions

A. From the group plot of mean reaction times as a function of memory set size, decide if the results confirm Sternberg's findings.

Discussion Questions

1. How would an exhaustive serial search work in comparison to a self-terminating serial search so that the exhaustive serial search was actually the more efficient of the two?

2. Some theorists have claimed that with appropriate assumptions it is possible to get a serial process to mimic a parallel one and vice versa. Try to design a parallel processor that behaves like a serial processor.

3. How likely is it that retrieval from short term memory always involves a serial exhaustive search?

Memory Processes – Encoding Specificty

According to the encoding specificity principle (Tulving, 1983) the recollection of an event depends on the interaction between the properties of the encoded event and the properties of the encoded retrieval information. In other words, whether an item will be remembered at a particular time depends on the interaction between the processing that occurred during encoding and the processing that occurs at retrieval.

This principle has important implications for what you can say about memory. Because it is the interaction of both encoding and retrieval that is important, it means that you cannot make any statement about the mnemonic properties of an item or a type of processing or a cue unless you specify both the encoding and the retrieval conditions (Tulving, 1983). Thus, you cannot say things like:

- Recognition is easier than recall
- Deep processing is better than shallow processing
- Pictures are recalled better than words

These statements are all meaningless because the encoding and retrieval conditions are not mentioned. It is easy to create situations in which recall is easier than recognition, shallow processing leads to better memory than deep processing, and words are recalled better than pictures.

This demo is based on Thomson and Tulving (1970). Some target words will be presented alone at study and some will be presented along with a weak cue. At test, there are three cue conditions: no cue, a weak cue, or a strong cue. A strong cue is a word that elicits a particular target word most of the time. For example, when most people hear the word DOG, the first word that pops into their head is CAT. A weak cue is a word that only rarely elicits a particular target. When people hear EYE, they respond with CAT only about 1% of the time. A reasonable prediction seems to be that strong cues should be better than weak cues at eliciting the correct item. However, this inference is not valid because it fails to take into account the relationship between the encoding and retrieval conditions.

There are two phases to this demo. Phase I. Start Phase I by pressing the space bar. You will see a series of words; each is shown on the screen for approximately 3 seconds. Some will be shown by themselves, and some as word pairs. For example, you might see: hand-PALM, or you might just see -PALM.

After all the words have been shown, you will be in Phase II. You will asked to judge whether the target word was one of the uppercase words you saw in Phase I. Sometimes you will see a target word shown by itself, and sometimes you will see it paired with a cue. For each uppercase word, press "Y" to indicate YES you did remember seeing the word in Phase I; press "N" to indicate that NO, you do not remember seeing the word. Press the space bar to start each test trial.

There are 48 words shown in Phase I and 96 trials in Phase II.

The summary results shows the proportion of times you responded Y (you remembered seeing the uppercase word during Phase I) to each of the nine conditions. You should find that when there was no cue present at study, you did best when there was a strong cue at test than either a weak cue or no cue. However, when there was a weak cue at study, you should find that the weak cue at test led to better performance than the strong cue. The important aspect of this result is that the effectiveness of even a long-standing strong cue depends crucially on the processes which occurred at study.

1. Why do you think that having a weak cue at the test phase improves the memory for a word that had a weak cue at study compared to a strong cue?

2. You are having trouble remembering your high school prom, although you know that you had a good time and it has only been 2 years. What could you do to try to remember your prom night?

3. While walking your dog, you see a strange dog running around. You think you remember seeing this dog before but you are not sure. As you round the corner, you run into a woman from your neighborhood that is looking for her dog. You suddenly remember that you saw that woman walking that strange dog you saw earlier in the week. What was missing when you were trying to remember if you recognized the stray dog?

4. While shopping for new cologne for your father for Christmas, you smell something that you recognize but you can't remember what the smell is. You find that you are having memory flashbacks of sitting around a fire and drinking apple cider with friends. As you look around, you notice a candle burning and you recognize that as the smell you detected. Explain how a candle you have never seen before could be related to the memory flashbacks with your friends.

5. You are a huge fraternity party and you see a girl playing beach volleyball that you think you recognize but you are not sure. You are not able to talk to her but it bugs you that you can't remember where you know her. On Monday morning as you walk into Biology class, you see that same girl sitting in front of you. You feel a bit stupid that you didn't remember her from the party because she has sat in front of you for 2 months now. Now that you have done this lab, how would you explain you memory problem?

Advanced Questions

A. While taking your psychology test, you notice that the girl beside you is singing a song about the different brain parts. After doing this lab, what could you infer about her encoding methods during her studying?

B. You find the morning of test day that the classroom has been changed from your regular classroom to a room that you have never been in. How do you think this will affect your test performance?

C. Your mother is making you your favorite pie for dessert, but she ran out of ingredients and asks you to go to the store for her. She only needs eggs, milk, white sugar and cinnamon, so you don't write it down. When you get to the store, you remember the milk, cinnamon and sugar but can't remember what the last thing was. Just then a woman walks in that is wearing the same shirt that your mother was wearing and you suddenly remember the eggs.

Discussion Questions

1. Now that you know that the environment and conditions where information is learned in plays an important role on memory recall or recognition, discuss some of the important factors to keep in mind if you were trying to study more effectively for a test.

2. Discuss how encoding specificity could be used to explain why using self-referent examples improve memory for to-be-learned material. Discuss any possible drawbacks with using your own examples over ones that teachers provide for you.

Memory Processes – False Memory

An important issue for theories of cognition is how well we remember things. It is important because nearly every aspect of cognition depends on memory to some degree. To understand problem solving, decision making, attention, and perception, one needs to know the abilities and limits of memory. The quality of memory is important for practical reasons as well. Many significant events depend on reports from human observers. From eyewitness testimony in murder trials to arguments with a spouse about who said what, memory, and memory accuracy, is critical. A surprising finding is that there is no way to assess memory accuracy without objective evidence (like a tape recording or a photograph). The vividness or confidence of the person recalling the memory is not an accurate indication of the truth of the memory. This is not to say that most memories are inaccurate; we must be pretty accurate much of the time or else living would be quite difficult. However, for those situations where accuracy of detail is important, memories cannot be trusted, no matter how adamant the recaller is about the vividness of the memory.

This experiment demonstrates one methodology that biases people to recall things that did not occur. The memories associated with experiments of this type are often called false memories. The method was first used by Deese (1959) and has been extended more recently by Roediger and McDermott (1995). The task is like many other memory experiments. A sequence of words is presented (verbally or visually) and the observer is to subsequently classify a set of words as either in the sequence (old) or not in the sequence (new).

What differentiates this experiment from other memory experiments is that the sequences are specially designed to bias observers to report a particular word that was not included in the list. When people report that one of these words was in the sequence, but it really was not, they are having a false memory. In some cases people will report that they vividly recall seeing (or hearing) the word, so their memory is very strong, despite its inaccuracy.

After clicking on the start button, a window will appear with a blank area on the left and a number of buttons on the right. Start a trial by pressing the Next trial button. On the left of the window a sequence of words will appear, with each word presented for one and a half seconds. After the full sequence has been presented, the buttons on the right will show labels for words, including some of those just shown. The other buttons will contain distracter words. You must distinguish the old words from the new, distracter, words. Your task is to click on the buttons for the words that were just shown. Not all the words in the sequence will be listed on the buttons. After you have finished clicking on all the buttons that you remember being in the sequence, click on Next trial to start the next sequence.

The experiment includes only six trials. For each trial click on the word buttons that were in the sequence just presented.

When the experiment finishes, a new window will appear that reports on three measures. First, it will report the percentage of times that you correctly selected an item that was in the sequence. Second, it will report the percentage of times that you (incorrectly) selected a distracter not presented, but not the special distracter. Third, it will report the percentage of times that you (incorrectly) selected the special distracter that was hypothesized to correspond to a false memory. You should find that the percentage of time you select the special distracter is larger than the percentage for other distracters and is smaller than the percentage for correct selections.

Results of this type can occur for more complex and meaningful memories as well. Loftus (1993) describes implanting a false memory in a teenager. With her method, the teenager developed a memory of being lost in a mall when he was five years old. After the initial implant, the teenager reported additional details of the event that were never suggested, and never happened. Research findings related to false memories should serve as a warning to therapists who try to recover "lost" memories. There is a danger that the therapist may implant a false memory rather than find a lost one.

Additional References

Brainerd, C. J. & Reyna, V. F. (1998). When things that were never experienced are easier to "remember" than things that were. *Psychological Science, 9,* 484-489.

Freyd, J. J. (1998). Science in the memory debate. *Ethics & Behavior, 8,* 101-113.

Hyman, I. E., Jr. Husband, T. H. & Billings, F. J. (1995). False memories of childhood experiences. *Applied Cognitive Psychology, 9,* 181-197.

Schacter, D. L. (1996). *Searching for memory: The brain, the mind, and the past.* New York: Basic Books.

Basic Questions

1. What is the difference between "special" and distracters that are "not special"?

2. Based on your experience of the word lists and the distracters, suggest a reason why these false memories might occur.

3. Do you think that there are any ways that we can help protect ourselves from false memories?

Advanced Questions

A. Look at the group results for each of three measures: mean percent of items presented in the sequence, non-special distracters not presented in the sequence, and special distracters not presented in the sequence. Decide if the false memory effect is confirmed.

Discussion Questions

1. Discuss the implications of this demonstration on claims about remembered past sexual abuse.

2. Discuss the idea that most of our memories must be fairly accurate or else living would be quite difficult.

3. Discuss the implications of the fact that we can be very certain about having a memory even though it is a false one.

Memory Processes – Forgot It All Along

There has been much controversy over the issue of recovered memories (for an excellent overview, see the book edited by Conway, 1997). This is the apparent finding that people who enter psychotherapy suddenly recover memories of events that happened to them years ago, usually memories of sexual abuse. Schooler, Bendiksen and Ambadar (1997) use the term discovered rather than recovered memories because the latter implies that the memories are of real events whereas the former is neutral on whether the memory is of a real event or not.

Schooler et al. (1997) note that there are three independent claims being made when a person in therapy discovers a memory:

1. The event that is remembered is a real event
2. The event was forgotten for a period of time
3. The event is suddenly remembered

Schooler et al. point out that these three elements are independent. For example, the event could be real and the memory could be accurate, but there might not have been a period during which the person was unaware of the event. Each of these claims can in principle be empirically evaluated.

Schooler et al (1997) found 4 cases in which they can demonstrate objectively (1) the original event occurred, (2) there was a period of time during which the person did not remember the event, and (3) the memory was suddenly discovered. What this demonstrates is not that all discovered memories are of real events, but rather that in at least some cases, a person can experience an event, can fail to remember that event, and then later can recall the event.

For the memory theorist, what is most interesting is the finding that at the time of discovery, the person has the experience of currently remembering the event but also believing they had not previously remembered the event. One explanation of this failure by people to remember that they had remembered has been termed the "forgot-it-all-along" effect (Schooler et al., 1997). [The name is based on the "knew-it-all-along" effect in which subjects who were told of a particular outcome over estimated what they would have known.] The basic idea is that during the discovered memory experience, the person thinks about the episode in a different way.

This demo is a laboratory analog of this "forgot-it-all-along" effect that was devised by Arnold & Lindsay (2002). No one is claiming that this is exactly the same effect as when people say they had not remembered being abused earlier but now they do. Rather, it is a demonstration that people can forget that they had remembered.

There are three phases. In Phase I, you will see a list of word pairs, a cue and a target. In Phase II, you will receive a cued-recall test. Sometimes the cue will be the same as in Phase I, and sometimes it will be different. In Phase III, you will be given a memory judgment task: you will be asked whether you recalled a target in the Phase II test. You should remember that you recalled an item better when the context is the same and you should forget that you recalled an item when the context is different.

There are three phases to this demo. Phase I. Start a trial by pressing the space bar. You will see a series of word pairs, such as cup-DESK. Each pair is shown for about 3 seconds. There are 88 pairs of words.

In Phase II, you will be given a cued recall test. You will be shown a cue and will be asked to recall the word that was presented with it. For example, you might see: cup-D--K. To respond, type in the two missing letters. If you can't remember the target, just type in any two letters. Press the space bar for the next test item.

In Phase III, you will be shown a cue and target pair again, but this time you will be asked whether you recalled the target in Phase II. Press "Y" to indicate YES you did remember it; press "N" to indicate that NO, you did not remember it. Press the space bar for the next test item.

There are 88 word pairs in Phase I, and 88 trials in Phase II and III.

Your performance on the cued-recall test should reflect the encoding specificity principle: You should do better when the context word at test (Phase II) is the same as during study (Phase I) than when it is different. Of more interest in this demo is the forgot it all along effect. When the context word presented during the memory judgment task (Phase III) was the same as during the cued-recall test (Phase II), you should have been more accurate in remembering that you remembered. In other words, you should have forgotten that you remembered the target word more often in the different context condition.

Basic Questions

1. In phase II of the lab, you had to fill in the missing 2 letters of the target word, which is what specific type of memory _____. Then in phase III, you had to respond either yes or no for each word shown as to whether you remembered the target word form phase II, which is what specific type of memory _____. Of the two specific types of memory, which is usually easier to do (greater accuracy)?

2. Think back to Phase II and the amount of time it took to fill in the missing letters of the target word and then to Phase III to the amount of time it took to say yes or no for each word. Which words took the greater amount of time to respond to? (Think in terms of the cue word that was paired with the target word)

3. After getting your mark for your philosophy test, you learn that a majority of the class failed. Your professor tells you not to worry that he will give you a second test and you can take the better of the two grades. Your performance on the second test was even worse than the first. As you are looking through your test, you found that you go things right the first time, but then got them wrong on the second test. How does this compare to the lab you just did?

4. Your best friend comes to in a panic and tells you about a guy who has been following you around campus all day trying to talk to her. As she is relaying her story, you suddenly have a flashback to your first year at the campus when some guy jumped out of the bushes at you when you were going to you car. Why did you think of the incident that occurred in you past?
    Answer: When your friend was telling you about her incident, it triggered your own personal memory when you were feeling vulnerable. This may have been the first time that you thought about the incident since it occurred.

5. While going downtown with your roommate, you find yourselves driving over a long bridge with water far below. When you look out of the window and down at the water you suddenly experience a weird feeling followed by a bout of panic. You've never experienced a fear of heights or bridges before so you mention this to your brother. He proceeds to tell the story of when the two of you were young and he pushed you off a log that ran over a creek in your backyard and you couldn't swim. Luckily your father pulled you out before you could drown. How could your sudden feeling of panic be explained?

Advanced Questions

A. The "forgot it all along" cognitive effect is similar to the physiological "opponent-process" effect. The opponent process occurs when your body learns the environment where you have an increased tendency to do drugs. Drugs, like cocaine put the body in an imbalanced state, so it learns to counteract this affect before hand (hence the name opponent). When you change environments but still take high levels of a drug (due to tolerance for the effect), the body isn't able to counter the effects of it and overdoses are common. Discuss how this opponent process is similar to "forgot it al along"?

B. When people get into serious accidents that involve traumatic head injuries, they can have problems remembering what happened to them before the accident. How might this be comparable to the repressed memories from bad childhood experiences?

Discussion Questions

1. We depend on our memories for a number of reasons in our society. Discuss some of the problems that affect our memories. Start with the major problems that are discussed in this lab and then think about other memory labs or information that you have learned from class. Be specific in your answers.

Memory Processes – Remember/Know

In a typical test of recognition memory, a subject might be shown a test item and asked whether it was one that was presented on a particular list. The target can be either old -- it was on the list -- or new -- it was not on the list. If the subject decides that an old test item was on the list, that is called a hit. If the subject decides that a new test item was on the list, that is called a false alarm.

A relatively recent change in testing recognition memory has been the introduction of the Remember/Know paradigm (Tulving, 1985). When subjects judge an item to be old, they are asked to make a further distinction. If they are consciously aware of some aspects of the original episode, then they should indicate that they remember the item. For example, they can remember a particular thought that the word triggered, or they can remember thinking it was a coincidence that this particular word followed the previous one. If they have no conscious awareness of the learning episode, then they should respond that they just know that the item was on the list.

The distinction can be explained in a different way. If you were asked, "Who was the first President of the United States?", you most likely would name George Washington. However, you probably do not consciously recollect the original episode during which you learned this information. Rather, you just know the answer. In contrast, consider the following statement: Abraham Lincoln's first vice-president was Hannibal Hamlin, who was born in Paris, Maine. If, later on, someone asks you, "Who was Abraham Lincoln's first vice-president?", you might answer with Hannibal Hamlin. If you were consciously aware that you first learned this fact while reading the CogLab CD student manual, then you would remember this information in the remember/know sense. Note that it is not the type of information that makes a difference; rather, it is the presence or absence of conscious awareness of aspects of the prior experience.

This demonstration replicates studies reported by Gardiner (1988) and Rajaram (1993). You will be shown a series of words, and asked to generate either a synonym or a word that rhymes. Then you will be given a recognition test, in which you will be asked to indicate whether you recognize the word.

Press the space bar to start each trail. There are two phases. You will need a blank sheet of paper and a pen for the first phase. In Phase I, you will see a word and an instruction. If the instruction says Synonym, write down a word that has the same meaning as the word shown. If the instruction says Rhyme, write down a word that sounds the same as the target word. When you are done, press the space bar for the next item. You will need to write down your work quickly: each item is shown for only 5 seconds.

After this, you'll enter Phase II. Press the space bar to start each trial. You will be shown a series of words, half of which were shown in Phase I, and half of which are new words. Please answer the question, Was this word in Phase I? If it was, decide whether you remember the word or simply know it was on the list. Press 'R' to indicate remember, and 'K' to indicate know. If the word was not on the list, press the 'N' key.

The judgment remember means that you are consciously aware of the learning episode: you can recollect some aspect of the experience, such as the word you provided as a synonym or rhyme, or the word that came before, or your thoughts about the word. If can't recollect such information, then you should choose know.

There are 80 words shown in Phase I, and 160 trials in Phase II.

When the experiment is over, you will see a table that shows how accurate you were in recognizing which items were on the original list. For the items that you said were on the list, you will also see the proportion of remember and know judgments made. You should give more remember than know judgments to words that you generated synonyms for, and you should give fewer remember and more know judgments to words that you generated rhymes for.

Additional References

Arnold, M. M., & Lindsay, D. S. (2002). Remembering remembering. *Journal of Experimental Psychology: Learning, Memory, and Cognition, 28*, 521-529.

Hyman, I. E., Jr., Gilstrap, L. L., Decker, K., & Wilkinson, C. (1998). Manipulating remember and know judgments of autobiographical memories: An investigation of false memory creation. *Applied Cognitive Psychology, 12*, 371-386.

Basic Questions

1. Why do you think "remembering" was related to the synonym condition & rhyming was related to "knowing?

2. When doing this lab, which task took a longer time to do (on average), coming up with a synonym or a rhyme?

3. Your friend just got a brand new sports car for his birthday and he said you could test drive it. All excited, you jump into the driver's seat and you notice that it is a standard. It has been a long time since you drove a standard. If you find yourself talking through the steps necessary to drive the standard as your father once told you, what kind of memory are you displaying and why?

4. During your psychology final exam you find you aren't really thinking very hard and you get through the multiple choice questions very quickly. You are the first one finished and although this worries you, you decide to leave to study for another final you have that afternoon. When you get your grade back for that test you see that you received a 90%. What kind of recognition memory was helping you through the test that quickly?

5. While at the mall, you see someone that you recognize, although you can't place why you recognize them. As they get closer to you, you hear her talking to a friend about playing in a band and you realize that she works at a music store near your house. How did knowing them change to remembering them?

Advanced Questions

A. You go into your favorite restaurant for supper and before you sit down, the waiter brings you an iced tea, your usual. How could you test what kind of recognition memory the waiter was using when he brought you the tea?

B. Exams are over and you are your roommates decide to rent a movie to unwind. They pick out a movie that you are positive that you haven't seen. As you start to watch the movie, something happens and suddenly you get excited and you know what the movie is all about. What has just happened to you?

C. Your roommate always sings in the shower and in the car on the way to school. In the shower, he just sings the songs from memory (no radio playing), but in the car, he sings along with the radio, even with those he is not too familiar with. Although he knows the words, he rarely knows what the words mean. Sometimes he makes more errors when he is familiar with the song. In terms of his memory, what could be happening?

Discussion Questions

1. Discuss any possible effects that level of <u>concreteness</u> or <u>abstractness</u> may play in your ability to "remember" a concept or "know" a concept. Talk about why this makes sense and use examples to support your answer.

2. One area of interest to memory researchers is the ability to manipulate memories through priming or leading. Discuss how this lab could contribute to the manipulation of "remembering" and "knowing" a memory. One of the references provided includes a study of manipulations of autobiographical memories.

Memory Processes – Serial Position

This demonstration explores effects of list position on free recall. In many instances we are presented with a list of items and must remember each of the items (e.g., grocery lists). If the order of the items is not required for accurate recall, the task is said to be unordered, or "free".

A general finding of free recall tasks is that recall of an item is strongly influenced by its position in a list. A common finding is that the last few items in the list are remembered best (called a recency effect), the first few items are remembered fairly well (called a primacy effect), but items in the middle of the list are not recalled very well at all. Surprisingly, this property holds for many types of items and for a wide variety of durations (seconds to years). The effect of serial position has played a major role in the development of memory theories.

Start a trial by pressing the Next trial button. The empty space on the left of the window will show a sequence of ten letters, each presented for one second. After the full sequence has been presented, the buttons on the right will become clickable. Your task is to click on the buttons that correspond to the letters in the sequence just shown in any order. You cannot click on more than ten buttons, and each button can only be clicked once for a given sequence. After you have finished clicking on all the buttons, click on Next trial to start the next sequence. The experiment includes fifteen sequences, with different letters making up the sequence each time.

Feel free to use whatever mental tricks you find help you recall the consonants. Some people mentally (or verbally) rehearse items to themselves. Some people also click on the buttons for the last few items in the list before they fade from memory.

You can also create variations of this experiment by changing what you do during presentation of the sequence, or how you report back items. For example, if you try to recall the letters in the sequence in the order they were presented, you will likely find that the recency effect disappears. If you repeat a phrase to yourself during presentation of the sequence, you will likely find that your overall performance drops.

When the experiment finishes, a new window will appear that plots the percentage of times you correctly recalled an item at each position in the sequence. You should find that you tend to have higher percentages correct for the first (serial position 1) and last (serial position 10) items in the list. For the middle positions (around serial position 5), you may find that your percentage correct is much lower.

Additional References

Bjork, R. A. & Whitten, W. B. (1974). Recency-sensitive retrieval processes in long-term free recall. *Cognitive Psychology, 6*, 173-189.

Greene, R. L. (1986). Sources of recency effects in free recall. *Psychological Bulletin, 99*, 221-228.

Postman, L. & Phillips, L. W. (1965). Short term temporal changes in free recall. *Quarterly Journal of Experimental Psychology, 17*, 132-138.

Rundus, D. (1971). Analysis of rehearsal processes in free recall. *Journal of Experimental Psychology, 89*, 63-77.

Tan, L. & Ward, G. (2000). A recency-based account of the primacy effect in free recall. *Journal of Experimental Psychology: Learning, Memory, and Cognition, 26*, 1589-1625.

Nairne, J. S., Neath, I., Serra, M., & Byun, E. (1997). Positional distinctiveness and ratio rule in free recall. *Journal of Memory and Language,* 37, 155-166.

Pinto, A. C., & Baddeley, A. D. (1991). Where did you park your car? Analysis of a naturalistic long-term recency effect. *European Journal of Cognitive Psychology*, 3, 297-313.

Basic Questions

1. Some theorists have suggested that the recency and the primacy effects in this demonstration is due to the operation of separate kinds of memory—long term and short term. Based on your experience with this demonstration, which effect probably comes from long term memory and which comes from short term memory?

2. Imagine that you have arrived at a party where you don't know anyone except the host. He introduces you to ten people all in a row by giving you their names. Later you would like to talk to some of them and be able to address them by name. What's your best strategy for whom to talk to first, last, and not at all?

3. What do you think would happen to the graph of the results of this demonstration if before you were allowed to recall the letters you were asked to do a few seconds of mental arithmetic?

Advanced Questions

A. Look at the group plot of the mean percentage of correctly recalled items as a function of serial position. Do the results in confirm the serial position effect?

Discussion Questions

1. The serial position effect can be obtained over durations of years. How does this fact complicate the idea that the recency and primacy effects are due to the operation of two separate memories?

2. Suggest some ways to improve recall for items on the middle of the list.

3. Rehearsal, which can explain the primacy effect, can be repeating items over and over again out loud or "in your head". Can you think of any other ways of performing rehearsal that might be effective?

Memory Processes – Von Restorff Effect

When people are trying to remember a set of items, events, or people, they often report being able to recall the information more easily and more accurately if the particular item is distinctive or stands out in some way from similar items. This type of result is usually known as the von Restorff effect, named after Hedwig von Restorff who published her results in 1933.

In the typical von Restorff experiment, you might see a list of 7 items and your task is to recall the items in their original order. In the control condition, you might see a list such as RMSKQLF. In the experimental condition you might see a list such as RMS4QLF. The typical finding is that you would be more likely to recall the digit 4 than the letter K. This effect is also sometimes known as the isolation effect because the 4 is isolated in the sense that it is the only digit. Research has shown that you can observe the von Restorff or isolation effect when the first item in the series is the different one. This rules out explanations based on differential encoding of the item because at the time the first item is seen, it is not different.

This experiment replicates classic results first reported by Pillsbury and Raush (1943). You will see lists made up of digits and letters. When there was only one digit in the list, recall of that item was excellent; as the number of digits increased and the number of letters decreased, recall of the digits decreased and recall of the letters increased. These results are now usually interpreted in terms of distinctiveness (Neath & Surprenant, 2003): the unusual (relative to the list) item stands out from the other items.

After clicking on the start button, a window will appear with a blank area on the left and a number of buttons on the right. Start a trial by pressing the Next trial button. On the left of the window a sequence of 8 items, either digits or letters, will appear, with each item presented for one second. After the full sequence has been presented, the buttons on the right will show labels for the items, including some of those just shown. The other buttons will contain distractor items. Your task is to click on the buttons for the items that were just shown. You are allowed to make only 8 responses; after you have clicked on 8 buttons, the remaining buttons will be disabled. After you have finished clicking on all the buttons that you remember being in the sequence, click on Next trial to start the next sequence.

The experiment includes 45 trials, 5 in each condition. For each trial click on the buttons to indicate which items were in the sequence just presented.

When the experiment finishes, a new window will appear that reports how well you recalled each type of list. You should find that in lists with 1 digit and 7 letters, you recalled the digit very well. As the number of digits increases, the recall advantage of the digits will decrease and the recall advantage of the letters will increase.

Additional References

Parker, A., Wilding, E. & Akerman, C. (1998). The Von Restorff effect in visual object recognition memory in humans and monkeys: The role of frontal/perirhinal interaction. *Journal of Cognitive Neuroscience, 10* (6), p. 691.

Main, K. M., Leland, L. M. & Bartlett, G. C. (1998). The properties of one: Facial memory and the isolation effect. *The Journal of General Psychology, 125*, (2), p. 192-207.

1. As you look at the graph depicting your results, you see that the proportion correct for the letter recall is at its highest when there were 7 digits and 1 letter. According to the lab, should your results be like this? Why or why not?

2. There is a set of identical twins, Judy and Jane, that sit next to you in your psychology class. You feel uncomfortable talking to them because you are constantly confusing them. A fellow classmate tells you a secret to telling them apart is a noticeable scar over one twin's eye. Why would this make sense after doing this lab?

3. You are having trouble trying to remember the different flowers that your grandmother has in her garden. The only one you remember is a rose bush but it is not your favorite flower. When you ask your mother, she recalls the rose bush too. If your grandmother has 10 plants in her garden that are about the same size and similar in color, why do you think you and your mother best remember the rose bush?

4. Why would it be good advertising scheme to have an upcoming rock star wear only one glove not two?

5. What would be the best way to remind motorists not to drink and drive and why? Putting signs about a no-tolerance policy for drinking and driving?
   a) Every 20 feet on the highway in the same color as the road signs, so people understand that it is an enforceable law
   b) Spread the signs around the community in bright letters or on signs that are a different color from other signs in the area.

6. Your friend takes you to a museum you have never been to before. You find yourself staring at a picture of a man who looks familiar but you have trouble recalling who it is. When your friend tells you that it is Winston Churchill you laugh because he is one of your heroes. Then you remember that the artist removed Mr. Churchill's cigar from his mouth when he painted his portrait. What is one possible explanation for why you did you not recognize Winston Churchill's face? (Use the Von Restorff Effect to support your answer)

Advanced Questions

A. Early Gestalt psychology used the figure/ground principle to explore the Von Restorff effect. How could the famous Rubin's vase (one way it looks like 2 faces and the other way it looks like a vase) be used to explain the isolation effect?

B. How is attention related to the Von Restorff Effect? Use specific examples to support your answer.

C. How could advertisers use the Von Restorff Effect to their advantage to increase the memory for their product?

Discussion Questions

1. You are designing a web page for your company. Researchers found that a memorable web site can increase sales by 60%. Taking what you have learned in this lab, what things could you incorporate into your web page. Give specific examples and the rationale behind them.

2. Using specific examples, discuss how the Von Restorff could be related to errors people make about unique events that occurred in their childhood?

Speech & Language – Categorical Perception - Identification

People perceive most stimuli continuously. For example, when you look at a rainbow, you see a smooth transition from red to yellow (like the image below):

You usually do not perceive stimuli categorically. Categorical perception means that you see either pure red or pure yellow and nothing in between (like the image below):

This is called "categorical" perception because instead of getting a percept that is ambiguous, you get a percept that perfectly matches an ideal example of a particular category. One thing that people seem to perceive categorically is speech (Harnard, 1987). What is interesting about this is that even when the physical stimuli change continuously (like the upper image), people perceive it categorically (like the lower image).

For example, both /b/ and /p/ are stop consonants: To produce these, you close your lips, then open them, release some air, and the vocal chords begin vibrating. Hold your hand in front of your mouth and say /ba/ and then /pa/. The difference between /ba/ and /pa/ is the time between the release of the air and the beginning of the vibration. This is referred to as voice onset time or VOT. For /b/, VOT is very short; voicing begins at almost the same time as the air is released. For /p/, the voicing is delayed.

Researchers can construct a series of stimuli in which the VOT changes in small steps. When people are asked to identify these stimuli, they generally have no difficulty: the first few are identified as /b/ and the second few are identified as /p/. What is most interesting is how the middle items are identified. Unlike most other stimuli, people do not report hearing something that is a bit like /b/ and a bit like /p/. Rather, they report hearing either /b/ or /p/.

To demonstrate categorical perception of speech stimuli, you really need two different measures. This lab provides one of those measures: it lets you find the point at which your percept changes from BA to PA through an identification task. The second (which is provided in the Categorical Perception - Discrimination experiment) examines your ability to tell whether two tokens are the same or different.

Before the demonstration begins, make sure the volume on your computer/speakers is set at a comfortable level. If you are running this lab in a public space, please use headphones so that you do not disturb other people.

Click once on the "Next Trial" button to hear a sound. Your task is to report what it most sounds like. Click once on the Ba button if you think the sound was most like Ba or click once on the Pa button if you think the sound was most like Pa.

Occasionally, the sound that is played might be distorted. If you did not hear the sound clearly, click once on the Redo button instead of on the BA or PA buttons. The trial will be repeated later on in the session. There are 10 trials for each stimulus, for a total of 90 trials.

At the end of the experiment, you will see how many times you labeled each stimulus as "BA". The typical result is to find that you labeled the first few items as "BA" 10 out of 10 times. You should also find that labeled the last few items as "BA" 0 out of 10 times. If you perceived the stimuli categorically, you should find that there is a quick drop in the number of times you labeled an item as "BA". The quicker the decrease (i.e., if you go from 10 out of 10 on stimulus 5 to 0 out of 10 on stimulus 6), the more categorical your perception.

Additional References

Cermak, L. S., Hill, R., & Wong, B. M. (1998). Effects of spacing and repetition on amnesic patients' performance during perceptual identification stem completion, and category exemplar production. *Neuropsychology, 12* (1), 65-77.

Postle, B. & Corkin, S. (1998). Impaired word-stem completion priming but intact perceptual identification priming with novel words: Evidence from the amnesic patient H.M. *Neuropsychologia, 36*, 421-440.

Stevenage, S. (1998). Which twin are you? A demonstration of induced categorical perception of identical twin faces. *British Journal of Psychology, 89*(1) p. 39-58.

Basic Questions

1. Why were the endpoints of the vocal continuum, "ba" and "pa" easier to identify than the sounds in the middle?

2. Where, in the stimuli continuum between "ba" and "pa", were more errors or misidentifications made?

3. While you are waiting to see your dentist, you notice a pretty picture in the corner of the reception area. It is hard to make out the detail from where you are sitting, but it looks like a moose in a swamp. As you walk towards it to get a better look, you suddenly stop because you now see two children playing on a beach. When you are right in front of the picture, you definitely see children on a beach. Describe what you have just experienced.

4. You are unloading groceries from the car when you hear music coming from the house. It sounds like, Help me Rhonda by the Beach Boys, and you start singing the chorus. When you get into the house, you don't think it is the Beach Boys and then you find out that it was really Jailhouse Rock by Elvis Presley. Your roommate thinks you should get your hearing tested so how can you put her mind at ease about what you thought you heard?

5. If the endpoints of two categories were "night" and "day", what is one constantly changing stimulus you could use to help you to identify whether it was night or day if you didn't have a watch?

Advanced Questions

A. What could you infer about categorical perception if a number of studies found that babies could identify categories, like mom and dad (or not mom) or their cat and dog?

B. While visiting a busy city, you have your wallet stolen. Based on your description, the police want you to look through a book of potential individuals to see if your thief was in there. You think that the people all look familiar, but you narrow it down to 3 people. How could reaction time be used to determine the reliability of your choices if the three faces took 5 seconds, 15 seconds and 25 seconds to identify as the potential thief?

C.   You have signed up to do a research project into perceptual identification that was using faces as stimuli. At one end is a typical female face and at the other end is a typical male face and there are slight facial morphs in between. What could the researcher use as dependent measures? What would each measure tell us about this psychological phenomenon?

Discussion Questions

1.   This lab explored the identification of sounds and the errors that we make. Do you think trained individuals, like a musician or conductor, would make fewer errors or would they be able to identify changes in sounds, tones or pitch more quickly than the non-trained person? Explain your answer.

2.   Explain how top-down (experience to physical stimuli) and bottom-up (physical stimuli to psychological experience) can influence our perceptual abilities? Examples may help to support your answer.

Categorical Perception – Discrimination

People perceive most stimuli continuously. For example, when you look at a rainbow, you see a smooth transition from red to yellow (like the image below):

You usually do not perceive stimuli categorically. Categorical perception means that you see either pure red or pure yellow and nothing in between (like the image below):

This is called "categorical" perception because instead of getting a percept that is ambiguous, you get a percept that perfectly matches an ideal example of a particular category. One thing that people seem to perceive categorically is speech (Harnard, 1987). What is interesting about this is that even when the physical stimuli change continuously (like the upper image), people perceive it categorically (like the lower image).

For example, both /b/ and /p/ are stop consonants: To produce these, you close your lips, then open them, release some air, and the vocal chords begin vibrating. Hold your hand in front of your mouth and say /ba/ and then /pa/. The difference between /ba/ and /pa/ is the time between the release of the air and the beginning of the vibration. This is referred to as voice onset time or VOT. For /b/, VOT is very short; voicing begins at almost the same time as the air is released. For /p/, the voicing is delayed.

Researchers can construct a series of stimuli in which the VOT changes in small steps. When people are asked to identify these stimuli, they generally have no difficulty: the first few are identified as /b/ and the second few are identified as /p/. What is most interesting is how the middle items are identified. Unlike most other stimuli, people do not report hearing something that is a bit like /b/ and a bit like /p/. Rather, they report hearing either /b/ or /p/.

To demonstrate categorical perception of speech stimuli, you really need two different measures. The first examines your ability to identify which sound you are hearing (and is provided in the Categorical Perception - Identification experiment). The second examines your ability to tell whether two tokens are the same or different. If you perceive the stimuli categorically, then it should be easy for you to correctly say that the tokens are different if they come from opposite sides of the category boundary. It should be very difficult for you to decide they are different if they come from the same side of the category boundary. In this lab, you will hear two sounds, and your task is to say whether they are the same or different.

Before the demonstration begins, make sure the volume on your computer/speakers is set at a comfortable level. If you are running this lab in a public space, please use headphones so that you do not disturb other people.

Click once on the "Next Trial" button to hear two sounds. Your task is to report whether they are the same or different. If you think they are the same, click once on the Same button. If you think they are different, click once on the Different button.

Occasionally, the sound that is played might be distorted. If you did not hear the sound clearly, click once on the Redo button; the trial will be repeated later on in the session. There are 140 trials.

At the end of the experiment, you will see a list of pairs of stimuli and how many times you labeled the pair as "Same". The typical result is to find that you labeled any comparisons between stimuli 1, 2, 3, and 4 as Same, and any comparisons between stimuli 6, 7, 8, and 9 as Same. This is because these stimuli all come from the same side of the category boundary. For comparisons that include stimuli from opposite sides of the boundary (especially comparisons between stimuli 4 and 6), you should find these labeled "Different".

Additional References

Levin, D. (2000). Race as a visual feature: Using visual search and perceptual discrimination tasks to understand face categories and the cross-race recognition deficit. *Journal of Experimental Psychology: General, 129*, p. 559-574.

Stark, C. & Squire, L. (2000). Intact visual perceptual discrimination in humans in the absence of perirhinal cortex. *Learning and Memory, 7(5)*, p. 273-278.

Basic Questions

1. What is the difference between "ba" and "pa" in terms of the voice onset time (VOT) that helps us to discriminate between these sounds?

2. According to the Coglab introduction, should stimuli 4 and 6 be determined as the same or different? Why or why not?

3. After reading through the literature, you discover that light blue is a calming color. You are having trouble sleeping, so you decide to paint your bedroom walls light blue. The salesclerk at the hardware store only has dark blue, but reassures you that she can make light blue by adding white paint to it. The clerk adds some white paint, but you still think it is a dark blue. She continues to add white paint, but you still think it looks like the same paint color she started with. The clerk adds the last bit of white paint she has and this time you think it is the light blue that you wanted. How could that small bit of white paint make a difference between dark and light blue paint?

4. Discuss the general problems that a color-blind person has discriminating between colors?

5. Your dentist is trying to determine the extent of damage you have in your wisdom tooth to see if it is worth saving or if he should pull it out. He pokes at your tooth in a sensitive spot and you jump in pain. On a scale from 1-10, you rate the pain as a 7. He continues to poke your tooth in different places and asks you each time if that was more painful or about the same amount of pain as the last poke. Explain how he is using categorical discrimination to determine the extent of the damage to your tooth?

Advanced Questions

A. Do you think it would be easier to discriminate between 5 and 10 pound weights or between 70 and 75 pound weights? Explain your answer.

B. What discrimination task would your optometrist use to determine if your eyesight had changed from –4.5 to –5.0?

C. You are trying to make juice, but you are not sure how much sugar should be used (the packages always tell you to put in more sugar than necessary). You decide to try adding a bit of sugar at a time and then tasting it to see if it is enough. You start off with 1/3 cup, but that is not enough; then another 1/3 cup, but you still can't taste a difference. After adding another 1/3 cup, you find it too sweet. Instead of adding another 1/3 cup the third time, what amount should you have added, knowing what you know about the boundary between sweet and sour?

Discussion Questions

1. Signal detection theory can be used to help explain the errors that we make in categorical perception. Discuss the four scenarios of signal detection (hit, miss, false alarm and correct rejection) to the errors and reaction time in discriminating between "ba" and "pa".

2. We have to socially discriminate between different categories of people, for example between honest/dishonest or funny/not funny. Although these characteristics follow a continuum, we don't usually describe someone as kind of honest or a bit funny? Give a specific example of a continuous behavior that we subjectively label as one way or another and discuss how we may be able to discriminate between the two categories. Don't use the examples already given. Indicate if setting the parameters between the 2 categories of behaviors is easy or hard to do and why.

Speech & Language – Lexical Decision

Theories of human language propose that there exists a mental dictionary, a lexicon, that contains a variety of information about words. This lexicon contains information about a word's meaning (its semantic content), its part of language (noun, verb, adjective, ...), and its relationships to other words (what can it follow?, what can follow it?, how can it be modified?). Psychologists are interested in the organization of this lexicon.

The lexicon is similar to a dictionary in that it holds information about words and other components of language. Physical dictionaries generally organize words alphabetically. This arrangement makes it easy to find any word, provided the spelling is known (or can be guessed). Because dictionaries are usually used to find the meanings of known words (or to check if a word is spelled properly), this organization is useful.

In the mental lexicon, though, the most useful feature of a word may not be its spelling, but its meaning, and its relationship to other words. If words are arranged in the lexicon by semantic relationships, then words that are related to each other (e.g., chair, seat, table, ...) would be close in the lexicon, while words that are unrelated to each other (e.g., chair, dinosaur, broccoli, ...) would be far apart.

Meyer and Schvaneveldt (1971) tested theories of this type using a lexical decision task. Words and pseudowords (e.g., "blar", or "plome") are presented and observers determine, as quickly as possible, whether or not the presented item is a valid word. Determining whether the item is a word involves searching the lexicon to see if the item is present. The time needed to make a "word" response indicates the time needed to search the lexicon to find the target word.

Meyer and Schvaneveldt hypothesized that search time would be shorter if the previously searched for word was close to the current target word. Search time would be longer if two successive words were in very different places in the lexicon. To test this hypothesis they presented pairs of items in sequence, and asked observers to judge each item in the pair as a word or nonword. They expected that the reaction time to the second item would be fastest if it was a word and the first item in the pair was a word that was semantically associated to the second item. The data showed exactly this effect.

You can find a similar effect searching through a physical dictionary, but with alphabetical order playing the important role. It will take less time to find the word "salivate" after searching for "salamander" and more time to find "salivate" after searching for "boomerang".

This experimental result has been taken as strong evidence for a class of theories based on spreading activation. These theories hypothesize that recognizing or thinking of a word involves activation of a node that codes that word. This activation spreads to nearby (semantically related) nodes, thereby priming those nodes and allowing faster response times in the lexical decision task. By running this type of task for many different types of words, one could, in theory, generate a description of semantic organization of the lexicon.

The results of this experiment are interesting for more than academic reasons. Many theories of language development and memory are based on spreading activation theories, and those theories have been used to motivate different treatments for a variety of learning problems.

After clicking on the start button, a window will fill the entire screen. Press the space bar to start a trial. After pressing the space bar, the screen will go dark and a small fixation square will appear in the middle of the screen. Fixate this square. Two to three seconds later, a word or nonword will appear above the fixation square. Decide if the item is a word or a nonword as quickly as possible. Press the / key if the item is a word. Press the z key if the item is not a word. The fixation square will turn red when you press either of these keys, so you will know your response has been recorded.

After making your decision, press the space bar. Two to three seconds later, a word or nonword will appear below the fixation square. Again, decide if the item is a word or nonword by pressing the z or / key as quickly as possible. You will receive feedback on whether you chose correctly.

After deciding on the item below the fixation square, press the space bar to start the next trial. There are at least 70 total trials. You must classify the items correctly for the trial to count, so if you find that you are making many classification mistakes, slow down. You can take a break after pressing the z or / key for the item below the fixation square; but do not press the space bar before taking the break. Pressing the t key will discard a trial (e.g., you sneeze or are otherwise interrupted). Discarded trials will be repeated later.

At the end of the experiment a window will appear that reports the reaction time to the second item for each of five cases. In the Associated case, both the first and second items are words, and the words are semantically related to each other. In the Unassociated case, both the first and second items are words, but they are not directly related to each other. In the other conditions one or both of the items is a nonword. You should find that reaction time is shorter for the Associated than the Unassociated case.

Additional References

Meyer, D. E., Schvaneveldt, R. W. & Ruddy, M. G. (1974). Loci of contextual effects in visual word recognition. In M. A. Rabbit & S. Dornic (Eds.) *Attention and performance V.* London: Academic Press.

Meyer, D. E., Schvaneveldt, R. W. & Ruddy, M. G. (1974). Functions of graphemic and phonemic codes in visual word-recognition. *Memory and Cognition, 2(2),* 309-321.

Neely, J. H. (1990). Semantic priming effects in visual word recognition: A selective review of current findings and theories. In D. Besner & G. Humphreys (Eds.) *Basic processes in reading: Visual word recognition.* Hillsdale, NJ: Erlbaum.

Ratcliffe, R. & McKoon, G. (1994). Retrieving information from memory: Spreading-activation theories versus compound-cue theories. *Psychological Review, 101,* 177-184.

Basic Questions

1. Using your experience with this demonstration, rate these 3 verbal items on their ability to facilitate recognition of "nurse" as a word. That is, imagine these 3 different items occurring as first items and in each case "nurse" follows. Your job is to decide as fast as possible that "nurse" is a word:

    question – nurse
    doctor – nurse
    plat – nurse

2. How could you use what you know about priming to give advice to people teaching children how to read?

3. How could you set up a lexical decision task in order to find out if "sheep" is more or less related to "lamb" compared to "wool"?

Advanced Questions

A. Use the group mean reaction times for the associated and unassociated cases to decide if Meyer and Schvaneveldt's results were confirmed.

Discussion Questions

1. Set up an experiment designed to discover the structure of that part of the mental lexicon that represents the words "garage", "car", and "gasoline".

2. Suggest some cognitive processes that rely on the mental lexicon.

3. Suggest some processes that might be involved in acquiring the mental lexicon. How is it learned?

Speech & Language – Word Superiority

Humans are miraculously good at recognizing visual patterns. Even the fastest of modern computers are nowhere near as efficient or thorough at identifying visual targets. How we acquired this level of sophistication is not fully understood. What is clear is that context plays an important role in interpreting a physical stimulus. We are not simply detectors of patterns of light; instead we infer interpretations of the physical stimulus.

The effect of context is made clear in a phenomenon called the word superiority effect (Reicher, 1969). In the experiment an isolated letter like K or a word like WORK is briefly flashed on a screen and then immediately replaced by a mask of X's and O's. The observer is then forced to choose between whether a D or a K was presented. A key component of the experiment is that either of the choices at the end of WOR would create a valid word. Thus, the observer's knowledge that the presentation contained a word does not automatically tell him which letter was presented. Even with this control, the experimental finding is that detection of K is better when it is part of a word than when it is presented in isolation. This is the word superiority effect.

This result seems paradoxical. In detecting an isolated letter, there is only one item to focus on. When a word is presented, more letters must be processed before the word can be detected. Thus, it would seem, detecting a letter in a word should be more difficult than detecting a letter in isolation. The data, however, demonstrates exactly the opposite effect.

This finding has been of significant interest to researchers that explore the processes involved in recognizing patterns. Although the word superiority effect has been a motivating result for a variety of theories, the effect has not been completely explained by any current theory. This demonstration allows you to participate in a version of the word superiority experiment.

After clicking on the start button, a window will appear to start the experiment. Start a trial by pressing the space bar. A fixation dot will appear in the middle of the window, stare at it. One second later a word or an isolated letter will briefly flash on the screen. The duration of this word or letter is very brief (approximately 40 milliseconds), then the word/letter is replaced with a mask of X's and O's. Half a second later, instructions will appear on which position you are to report on. These instructions are of the form *---S or M? This indicates that you are to report on whether the letter in the first position is an S or an M. An instruction like --*- E or L? indicates that you are to report on whether the letter in the third position was an E or a L. Simply type in the letter that you saw at the indicated position. You will not receive any feedback on whether your guess was correct. The letter you type, however, will be shown in red on the bottom half of the screen. This indicates that the computer has registered the key you pressed.

You may find that in some trials you have no idea what the queried letter was. In those cases, just guess one of the options. (You may find that on the isolated letter trials you see a letter but it is in a different place than you are queried. Guessing that letter might be a good strategy because with these brief duration's, things sometimes seem to jump around.)

Press the space bar to start the next trial. If you wish, before pressing the space bar, but after identifying the letter, you can check how many trials remain for the current experiment with the Trials to go pull-down menu.

There are a total of 96 trials. There are 16 four-letter words and 16 isolated letters in different locations. Each condition is repeated three times. If you respond before the probe appears, the trial will be repeated later.

At the end of the experiment a new window will appear that reports the percentages of correct detection's in the word trials and the isolated letter trials. You should find that the percentage is larger for the detection of a target letter in a word than in isolation. If you are truly guessing on each trial, then your percentages should be close to 50%.

Additional References

Forster, K. I. (1981). Priming and the effects of sentence and lexical contexts on naming time: Evidence for autonomous lexical processing. *Quarterly Journal of Experimental Psychology, 33A*, 465-495.

Jordan, T. R. & Bevan, K. M. (1994). Word superiority over isolated letters: The neglected case of forward masking. *Memory & Cognition, 22*, 133-144.

Richman, H. B. & Simon, H. A. (1989). Context effects in letter perception: Comparison of two theories. *Psychological Review, 96*, 417-432.

Basic Questions

1. Do your results indicate a word superiority effect? Explain your answer.

2. What do you think would happen on trials where letters were presented in non-words? For instance, you are given EMESD and asked to report the letter in the last position. How would performance compare with D presented by itself or in a word like HEARD?

3. A "sentence superiority effect" has been demonstrated for words. What would this effect be?

Advanced Questions

A. Look at the group mean percent correct detections for the word trials and the isolated letter trials. Do the results confirm the word superiority effect?

Discussion Questions

1. What general implications does the word superiority effect have for our understanding of the reading process?

2. How do you think the word superiority effect might change with age? Why?

3. How would reading be different if the word superiority effect didn't exist?

Concepts – Absolute Identification

Lots of research in cognitive psychology has focused on whether there is a fundamental limit on people's capacity to process information and, if so, what that limit is. It might often seem that we have almost unlimited potential, especially when it comes to identifying and recognizing different items. Think of all the different people you can identify, or cars, or animals, or buildings, or pieces of furniture. Given the ease with which all of these items can be identified, it comes as a surprise to most people to find that when items vary in just one dimension, they cannot identify even seven items. The research that demonstrates this limitation is often done using a procedure known as absolute identification.

In a typical absolute identification experiment, people are exposed to a set of stimuli that vary systematically along only one dimension (e.g. nine tones of different frequencies, or eight lines of different lengths). A label, often a digit, is associated with each stimulus. The task is simply to produce the correct label in response to the presentation of an item from the set.

When the items are evenly spaced, the first and last items in the series are identified most easily. In contrast, identification of the middle items is usually quite poor. Such effects are found for many dimensions, such as frequency, loudness, weight, area, line length, and semantic continua.

One curious aspect is that performance seems fundamentally limited: no matter how many trials you get, you never get perfect at this task as long as the stimuli vary along only one dimension (Shiffrin & Nosofsky, 1994). If the stimuli varied along two or more dimensions, the task becomes trivially easy. For example, you probably have no trouble identifying the letters in the alphabet.

This is because the letters vary on multiple dimensions including height (the letter 't' is taller than the letter 'e'), curvature (the letter 'i' is straight, the letter 's' is all curves), and others.

When the demonstration begins, you will see a new window appear. Press the space bar to start a trail.

The first time through, you will see all of the lines presented together from 1 (the shortest) to 7 (the longest). This will give you an idea of what the lines look like.

For the rest of the trials, you will see one of the 7 lines presented in the middle of the screen. Your task is press a key that indicates which line you think it is. For example, if you think it is Line 2, press the 2 key. If you think it is Line 6, press the 6 key. The computer will tell if you were correct. If you were not correct, the computer will also tell which line it was.

You start each trial by pressing the space bar. There are 70 trials, which sounds a lot, but it takes only a couple of seconds per trial.

When the experiment finishes, a new window will appear that shows you how well you identified each line length. For example, to see the number of times Line Length 3 was identified as Line Length 5, find 'Line 3', in the first column, and 'Line 5' in the first row, and then find the number where the row and column intersect. You should find that performance is worse for the middle item (Line 4) and is better as you get nearer the end stimuli. Furthermore, you should find that when you make a mistake, you are most likely to select an item very close to the correct item.

Additional References

Lacouture, Y. (1997). Bow, range and sequential effects in absolute identification: A response-time analysis. *Psychological Research, 60*, 121-123.

Rouder, J. (2001). Absolute identification with simple and complex stimuli. *Psychological Science, 12* (4).

Harbensak, G, (1992) The consistency model: A process model for absolute judgment. *Journal of Experimental Psychology: Human Perception and Performance. 18,* 303-309.

Miller, G. A. (1956). The magical number seven plus or minus two: Some limits on our capacity for processing information. *Psychological Review,63 ,81-97.*

Siegel, J. A. & Siegel, W. (1977). Absolute identification of notes and intervals by musicians. *Perception and Psychophysics, 21,* 143-152.

Basic Questions

1. Would it make sense if the class results revealed that a majority of misidentification errors were found between line 4 and 5? Explain your answer.

2. Would the line identification task have been easier if the lines varied on length and thickness, where line 7 would have been the thickest and line 1 was the thinnest?

3. You are watching your favorite gardening show and the host is talking about wedding flower arrangements. All of the flowers she is using are pink with varying blooms. When the flower arrangement is completed your roommate walks in and starts watching the program with you. She asks for the name of one particular flower and you say that it is one of three possibilities, but you are not absolutely sure which one it is. How could you explain your inability to determine exactly which of the three flowers it was?

4. You are new to campus and you're trying to find your way around, although you are having trouble finding the psychology building. You stop a passing student and ask them if they know where Vari Hall is (psychology is housed in this building). They point over your shoulder to the right and tell you it is the tall building and walk away quickly. When you look in the pointed direction you see 5 identical buildings, but 3 look to be taller than the other 2. Why will you have trouble identifying Vari Hall?

5. In a study that you are doing, you have to taste 7 dark brown fluids and rank them from 1-7 for their sweetness, with 7 being the sweetest and 1 being not at all sweet. After tasting all 7, you start to rank them, immediately setting drink C in position 1 and F in position 7. Why were these positions the easiest to determine? Which positions might be the hardest to rank? Why?

Advanced Questions

A. For your summer break, you decide to travel to South Africa to do some volunteer work in a remote village. The males of this tribe look identical except for a decorative bone they wear in their nose lengthways. You are told that the length of the bone correlates with the man's status, the longer the bone, the greater the status. It is important that you learn each man's status within the tribe so you can greet him accordingly. What kind of problems could you encounter with this task?

B. For Christmas, your mother bought you a clock that chimes like a tugboat on the hour. At 12:00, the tugboat toots goes on for 24 seconds and at 1:00 the chimes last for 2 seconds. If you were trying to tell the time by the tooting, what kinds of problems could you face? Give specific examples of potential problems.

C. Come up with an example, using the volume range on a stereo system from 1-10, with 1 being the lowest and 10 being the loudest setting. In this example, describe the problems with absolute identification of volume level as well as the conditions that need to apply for this phenomenon to be considered. Be creative.

Discussion Questions

1. Discuss how the results of this lab contribute to the idea that humans have a limited capacity for processing information.

2. The concept of Absolute Identification has been applied to cross-cultural errors in identifying people. For example, errors increase when a Caucasian tries to identify a Chinese person. Discuss how the increased errors could be explained.

Concepts – Implicit Learning

The term implicit learning refers to "the process by which knowledge about the rule-governed complexities of the stimulus environment is acquired independently of conscious attempts to do so" (Reber, 1989, p. 219).

One form of implicit learning involves serial pattern learning. In this task, subjects are asked to press one of four keys as quickly as they can whenever they see an stimulus, such as an asterisk, appear in any of four locations (labeled A, B, C, and D). If the asterisk appears in location A, the subject is asked to press (for example) the "z" key. If the asterisk appears in location B, the subject is asked to press the "x" key. There is an underlying pattern that defines the order of locations. It is this pattern that the subject will learn.

As the sequence is repeated, subjects press the keys more quickly. This indicates that learning has taken place. More evidence comes from a transfer test, in which the pattern is changed (again, without telling the subject). Now, the subjects press the keys much more slowly.

The key evidence to support the idea that learning is implicit -- not conscious -- comes from tests in which subjects are asked what the pattern was. The typical finding is that subjects are unaware of the pattern, but their behavior shows that they have nonetheless learned it (see Stadler & Frensch, 1998).

This demonstration is modeled on a study reported by Destrebecqz and Cleeremans (2001). There will be a long series of trials in which you will be asked to indicate the location of a circle. Please try to respond as quickly as you possibly can. At the end of the experiment, you will be asked what the rule was that determined the circle's location.

After clicking on the start the button, a window will appear. Start a trial by pressing the space bar. A short time later, a circle will appear in one of the four locations shown below. Your task is to indicate the location of the circle by pressing the appropriate key as quickly as you can.

- If the circle appears in the left-most location, press the "z" key as quickly as you can.
- If the circle appears in the second location, press the "x" key as quickly as you can.
- If the circle appears in the third location, press the "." key as quickly as you can.
- If the circle appears in the right-most location, press the "/" key as quickly as you can.

Place your left index finger on the "x" key and your right index finger on the "." key. Place your left middle finger on the "z" key and your right middle finger on the "/" key.

If the '.' and '/' keys are not the right-most keys on your keyboard, you can use the Instructions menu that will appear once you start the demo. There are 288 trials (each trial takes only a few seconds), and you can take a rest every 24 trials. Press the space bar to start each trial.

At the end of the experiment a new window will appear that reports the mean reaction time (RT) in milliseconds for each block of 24 trials. You should find that your mean RT decreases with each block. On Block 10, you should find a sudden increase in mean RT because that block uses a different pattern. Blocks 11 and 12 go back to the first pattern. Before you look at the results window, try to write down what the pattern was that determined the order of the locations. Then, compare your "rule" with the one provided in the window. You should find that your "rule" is incorrect even though your RTs show that you learned the rule!

Additional References

Advertising

Shapiro, S. & Krishnan, H. (2001). Memory-based measures for assessing advertising effects: A comparison of explicit and implicit memory effects. *Journal of Advertising, 30* (3).

Development

Vinter, A. & Perruchet, P. (2000). Implicit learning in children is not related to age: evidence from drawing behavior. *Child Development, 71* (5), p. 1223.

Motor skills

Pohl, P., McDowd, J., Filion, D., Richards, L. & Stiers, W. (2001). Implicit learning of a perceptual-motor skill after stroke. *Physical Therapy, 81*, p. 1780-1790.

Amnesia

Curran, T. (1997). Higher-order associative learning in amnesia: Evidence from the serial reaction time task. *Journal of Cognitive Neuroscience*, 9 (4), p. 522-534.

Basic Questions

1. If the results show the mean reaction times gradually decreasing from block 1 to block 12, what could one imply was happening?

2. Indicate which of the following examples would be explained through explicit or implicit learning. Just write explicit or implicit in the space provided.
    a) Driving a standard vehicle _____
    b) Arriving 10 minutes late to a class where the professor is usually 15 minutes late

    _____

    c) Being able to sing along with your favorite song, but not being able to write out the words

    _____

    d) Answering these questions _____
    e) You have trouble writing down directions to your Grandmother's house, but you are able to drive out there with no problems _____

3. Through Classical Conditioning, a neutral stimulus (like cologne) can elicit or bring about a positive emotional response when we learn to associate it with someone we like, for example our boyfriend or girlfriend. How can this association be explained in terms of implicit learning?

4. Your friends are talking about a song that you insist you do not know. Even after hearing part of the song, you still don't recognize it. When the chorus comes along, however, you start to sing the words. Now your friends think you were lying to them. How could you explain this behavior using implicit learning?

5. While driving to school, you stop to give your friend a ride. While driving, your friend asks why you take the Hospital route when University Avenue is faster. You really don't know why you take the Hospital route, but you have been doing it since last year around Christmas time. Could implicit learning be used to explain why you take the longer route? What if you knew that there was construction on University Avenue that began around Christmas time that held up traffic going to the University?

6. How do advertising companies use the concept of implicit learning when designing their client's commercials?

Advanced Questions

A. In a recent Hollywood film, <u>Momento,</u> the main character received a blow to the head and developed Anterograde amnesia. He could not for new long-term memories and lost all personal memories from the time of the accident to the present, however, he could use a telephone, drive a car, walk and talk. From this information, what would you suspect about the type of memory loss related to Anterograde amnesia?

B. Is the concept of either having two separate memory stores or at least two aspects of one main memory system important to understanding human behavior.

C. How can implicit learning be used to possibly explain an addiction to alcohol?

Discussion Questions

1. Give 3 specific examples of odd behaviors you exhibit and then think about possible explanations for these behaviors. Use the concepts of implicit and explicit learning to answer this question.

2. How would implicit memory be related to some psychological disorders, like obsessive-compulsive disorder, bipolar (or other mood disorders), eating disorders or anxiety disorders? Discuss specific behaviors related to a disorder and how learning could allow the abnormal behavior to continue.

Concepts – Mental Rotation

When we carry out some cognitive tasks we seem to use mental images. For example, how many windows are in your house or apartment? To answer this question most people seem to recall a mental map of their apartment and, mentally, move through the map as they count windows.

Although everyone seems to experience something that we call mental imagery, it is difficult to draw conclusions from such introspections. For example, some people report that their mental images are very sketchy and ill defined, while others report their mental images are detailed and crisp. Based solely on these reports, it is impossible to know whether people's mental images really differ, or if some subjects just describe the mental images differently.

To explore mental images more objectively, researchers give subjects tasks that seem to require the use of mental images. As a critical part of the task is varied, some characteristics of mental images can be deduced. Roger Shepard and his colleagues (e.g., Shepard & Metzler, 1971) designed one of the most often used tasks. In this task subjects were shown two novel visual stimuli and were asked to determine whether the stimuli had the same shape or different shapes. The shapes (random block shapes) were rotated either in the plane or in depth. Subjects reported that they mentally rotated an image in their head until the two stimuli were oriented the same way, and then made their judgment.

When subjects were asked to make their response as quickly as possible, the reaction time increased with the angle of rotation between the shapes. This suggests that it takes time to mentally rotate an image, and implies that mental images are much like real images. Shepard further found that every 50 degrees of physical rotation required one second of mental rotation before subjects could respond. This suggests that the rate of mental rotation is at a constant velocity.

Shepard's findings have had a large influence on theories of mental representation. This experiment allows you to participate in a variation of the mental rotation task.

Start a trial by pressing the space bar. Two random shapes will appear on the screen, one to the left and one to the right. The two shapes are either identical, or one is a mirror image of the other. One shape is also rotated clockwise 0, 45, 90, or 135 degrees relative to the orientation of the other shape. Your task is to determine whether the two shapes are mirror images or not. Respond as quickly as possible by pressing the z key (for "mirror") or the / key (for "not mirror"). You will receive feedback on whether you were correct. When you are ready for the next trial press the space bar again.

There is a minimum of 80 trials. For each "mirror" and "not mirror" condition 10 trials are presented for each rotation angle. If you make a mistake (e.g., say the stimuli are mirrors when they were not), the trial will be repeated (with different stimuli) later in the experiment. In this way, only reaction times where you were correct are used. If you find you are often making mistakes, you should try slowing down on your responses and/or try harder.

When you finish the experiment a window will appear that plots reaction time as a function of rotation angle, with separate curves for "Mirror" and "Same" trials. You should find that both curves increase with rotation angle, and that the curves are nearly straight lines.

Additional References

Biederman, I. & Gerhardstein, P. C. (1993). Recognizing depth-rotated objects: Evidence and condition for three-dimensional viewpoint invariance. *Journal of Experimental Psychology: Human Perception and Performance, 19,* 1162-1182.

Cooper, L. A. (1975). Mental rotation of random two-dimensional shapes. *Cognitive Psychology, 7,* 20-43.

Cooper, L. A. (1976). Demonstration of a mental analog of an external rotation. *Perception and Psychophysics, 19,* 296-302.

Cooper, L. A. & Shepard, R. N. (1973). The time required to prepare for a rotated stimulus. *Memory and Cognition, 1,* 246-250.

Basic Questions

1. Extend Shepard and Metzler's findings to another imagery task. What would they predict about how long it would take to say how many windows were in a familiar room in which the windows were far apart from each other vs. how many windows were in a familiar in a room in which the windows were close together?

2. Some of you may not have obtained straight lines for the graph of the results or you may not have found that reaction times increase as angle of rotation increases. Give some reasons why this might have happened.

3. Describe an every day task that might depend on the same abilities that you used to do this demonstration.

Advanced Questions

A. Use the plot of mean group reaction times as a function of angle of rotation for "mirror" and "same" trials to see if the results confirm Shepard and Metzler's findings.

Discussion Questions

1. Practice improves performance on mental rotation tasks. How might this happen?

2. Do you think there is any other way of explaining Shepard and Metzler's findings that doesn't rely on mental rotation?

3. Create a short set of instructions using mental rotation techniques to help someone trying to improve an athletic skill like shooting baskets or serving in tennis or anything else that you can think of.

Concepts – Prototypes

Part of cognitive psychology explores the concept of concepts. What cognitive events happen when you think about a chair? How is the concept of chair represented in the cognitive system? This is a subtle issue. For example, surely a seat at a formal dining table is chair, but what about a recliner, a stool, a couch, or a tree stump? The issue is important because the representation of concepts is the basis of everything else we can mentally do with concepts. In a very real sense how we think and what we can learn is largely determined by how we represent concepts.

An efficient way to represent concepts would be to keep only the critical properties of a concept. This set of critical properties is sometimes called a prototype or schema. The idea of prototypes is that a person has a mental construct that identifies typical characteristics of various categories. When a person encounters a new object he/she compares it to the prototypes in memory. If it matches the prototype for a chair well enough the new object will be classified and treated as a chair. This approach allows new objects to be interpreted on the basis of previously learned information. It is a powerful approach because one does not need to store all previously seen chairs in long term memory. Instead, only the prototype needs to be kept.

This experiment allows you to participate in a type of experiment that is often used to investigate the creation and storage of concepts. It is a variation of a method used by Posner and Keele (1968), which is one of the earliest studies to systematically explore concept representation in a controlled way. Rather than using an already well-known concept like a chair, Posner and Keele had participants learn patterns of dots. The patterns were variations of a few prototypes, but the prototypes themselves were not seen during a training phase. During the training phase participants learned to classify the variations, with the underlying prototype being the basis for correct classifications.

After learning to classify the variants, participants were shown a variety of dot patterns. In particular, they were shown patterns that were shown during the training phase, new variant patterns, and the patterns corresponding to the prototypes. Classification and reaction time performance were nearly equal for the previously seen variants and the prototypes. Performance was slightly worse for the new variants. This is significant because both the new variants and the prototypes were never seen during testing. To classify dot patterns that were not previously seen, the participants must be using a mental concept of what corresponds to the different categories. Since performance is better for the prototype patterns than for the new variants, the mental concept is similar to the prototype patterns. The conclusion seemed to be that people created a mental representation that was a mixture of the variant patterns used during training, that is, a prototype.

Posner and Keele's experiment led to an intense investigation on concept formation and representation. Much of that research is consistent with prototype theories. However, there are aspects of the experimental data (even in Posner and Keele's experiment) that suggest that the prototype theories cannot be the sole basis for concept representation. For example, our behavior is often influenced by the properties of individual experiences, and some theories of concept formation suggest that this alone can account for the data purported to imply prototypes. Nevertheless, prototypes are a part of many theories of cognition in a variety of forms. This demonstration is a variation of Posner and Keele's experiment.

After clicking on the start button, a window will appear that fills the screen. Press the space bar to start a trial. After the bar press a fixation point will appear for a second and then will be replaced by randomly placed dots. Your task is to classify the dot pattern as z or as / by pressing those respective keys. On the first few trials you will not be able to properly classify the patterns, but you will receive feedback on each trial and so can learn which pattern corresponds to which keypress. You should make your responses as quickly as possible, but try to be accurate.

The experiment consists of separate training and testing phases. The training phase includes at least 60 trials (trials where a mistake is made are repeated later in the experiment) and the testing phase contains at least 30 trials. Each dot pattern in the training phase is a variation of one of two fixed prototype random dot patterns. The variations are made by randomly taking ten of the twenty-five dots in a prototype and moving them to a new position.

After completing the training phase, a new set of dot patterns is presented. The transition from training to testing is fairly seamless, and you might not notice when it happens. The dot patterns in the testing phase are of six types. One is the prototype that corresponds to the classification of z. Another is the prototype that corresponds to the classification of /. The other four patterns are new variations of these prototypes (two variations for each prototype). Each dot pattern is presented five times in random order.

Throughout this experiment your task is always the same. As quickly as possible classify the pattern as z or /. Press the space bar to start the next trial.

At the end of the experiment a new window will appear that reports the average reaction time (in milliseconds) to classification of the dot patterns in the testing phase. You should find that the reaction time to the prototype patterns is faster than the reaction time to the new variants.

Additional References

Reed, S. K. (1972). Pattern recognition and categorization. *Cognitive Psychology, 3,* 382-407.

Smith, E. E. & Medin, D. L. (1981). *Categories and concepts.* Cambridge, MA: Harvard University Press.

Solso, R. L. & McCarthy, J. E. (1981). Prototype formation of faces: A case of pseudomemory. *British Journal of Psychology, 72,* 499-503.

Basic Questions

1. Try to extend the idea of prototype to an every day concept such as "college or university student". What might characterize the prototypical college or university student?

2. Look at your data and decide if they are what Posner and Keele would have predicted. There's one measure not included in the demonstration that Posner and Keele made. What is it and how big should it be in relationship to the measures you did make?

3. What sorts of cognitive work might prototypes be useful for?

Advanced Questions

A. Look at the group mean reaction times for classification of prototypes and for classification of new variants. Do this by grouping the data for both prototypes together and for all four new variants together. Decide if Posner and Keele's results were confirmed.

Discussion Questions

1. Prototypes are mental constructions. Suggest how the construction process might take place.

2. If prototypes are used to classify incoming patterns of stimulation some sort of matching process between the prototype and the incoming stimulus must take place. Describe how the matching process might work.

3. Describe the characteristics of a prototype. What makes it a prototype?

Judgment – Monty Hall

Most people have a poor understanding of probability. One common problem occurs when evaluating combinations of events. The Monty Hall 3 Door problem is a classic example. Based on an old TV game show, Let's Make A Deal, the problem involves 3 doors. Behind one of the doors is a prize. The contestant picks one door. Monty Hall, the eminent emcee, picks one of the remaining two doors to open and shows that the prize is not there. The question is: Do you stay with your original pick or do you change your pick? (We assume Monty Hall is playing fair and always does this.)

You originally begin with a 1 in 3 chance (0.333 probability) of picking the correct door. Many people think that it doesn't matter whether you stay with your original pick or switch after Monty reveals his door.

This interpretation is incorrect. You are better off always switching; over the long term, you will average 66% correct. If you always stay, you will average 33% correct over the long term. If you randomly switch or stay, you will average 50% over the long term.

Here's how to think of it. You begin with a 1 out of 3 chance of picking the correct door. Monty Hall shows that one of the other doors is incorrect. If you do nothing, you still have a 1/3 chance of being correct. Because you know the prize is not behind the door he opened, it must be behind the remaining door 2/3 of the time and behind the door you picked 1/3 of the time.

This lab simulates the Monty Hall 3 Door Problem. It lets you try out the various options and see how often you would win. Start a trial by clicking on the Next Trial button. Then, select a door. One of the doors will have its contents changed from '?' to '-' to indicate there is no prize. Now, you decide whether to pick your original door again, or whether to switch. Once you either confirm your original choice or pick a new door, the winning door will be shown (with a '+') the other losing door will be shown (with a '-').

To maximize the number of wins, make your first selection randomly, and then always change to the other door. To minimize the number of wins, make your first selection randomly, then always stick with your first choice.

When the experiment finishes, a new window will appear that shows you how many times you successfully picked the winning door. If you randomly picked a door, and then randomly switched or stayed, you should be right 50% of the time. If you randomly picked a door and stayed with that choice, you should be right 33% of the time. If you randomly picked a door and always changed, you should be right 66% of the time.

Additional References

Bailey, H. (1999). Monty Hall uses a mixed strategy. *Mathematics Magazine, 73* (2), 135-141.

Eisenhauer, J. G. (2000). The Monty Hall Matrix. *Teaching Statistics, 22* (1), 17-20.

Fernandez, L. & Piron, R. (1999). Should She Switch? A Game-Theoretic Analysis of the Monty Hall Problem. *Mathematics Magazine, 72 (3)*, 214-217.

Friedman, D. (1998). Monty Hall's three doors: Construction and deconstruction of a choice anomaly. *The American Economic Review, 88,* 933-946.

Baron, J. (1988). *Thinking and deciding.* Cambridge, UK: Camridge University Press.

Kahneman,D. & Tversky, A. (1973). On the psychology of prediction. *Psychological* Review, *8, 237-251*

Von Winterfeldt, D. & Edwards, W. (1986). On cognitive illusions and their implications. In H. R. Arkes& K. R. Hammond (Eds.) *Judgment and decision making: an interdisciplinary reader. Cambridge, UK:* Cambridge University Press.

Basic Questions

1. Why does the probability of winning increase from a 1 in 2 chance to a 2 in 3 chance when you always switched doors in the lab?

2. If a situation has 2 possible outcomes, what is the chance level or the possibility of an event occurring by chance?

3. While you were doing the lab, what would you start to think if you lost 10 times in a row? Are the losses independent or dependent of one another?

4. In the game show, "Let's Make a Deal", it was imperative that Monty Hall knew where the grand prize was so he could reveal the other losing curtain. In terms of probability, why was this imperative?

5. According to the Monty Hall principle, what should you do in the following scenario?
   "You are dating three potential females (Brenda, Stephanie and Heather) because you are looking for the perfect woman to marry. You've heard that 2/3 of all marriages end in divorce, so you want to be sure that you are that 1 couple that makes it. You decide to marry Brenda and break Stephanie and Heather's hearts. Two years later you hear that Stephanie married a friend of yours right after you broke up with her, but it recently ended in divorce. What do you do, stay with Brenda or look for Heather's phone number?

Advanced Questions

A. Your psychology professor tells the class that 1/5 of the class will fail her class because it is tough and requires a lot of work. If there are 200 people in her class, how many people will fail if her statistic is correct?

B. What would the probability of winning the grand prize be if there were 7 curtains or doors instead of 3 to begin with, but he revealed the prizes behind 2 doors?

Discussion Questions

1. Humans have problems understanding probabilities of events occurring. Discuss some of the reasons why we have these problems. For example, could these problems be due to a misunderstanding of the problem or limitations of our brains? Give examples to help support your answer.

2. The Monty Hall problem sparked a debate for a number of years among the highly intellectual academics. What do you think some of the possible reasons are for the heated debate? Discuss the problem itself and not the stubborn nature of academics.

Judgment– Risky Decisions

Our lives are full of decisions. We must choose what books to read, movies to see, courses to take, person to date, routes to drive, and thousands of other decisions every day. You might hope that people weigh their options carefully and make the best decision possible. Studies in cognitive psychology, however, tell us that the way people make decisions is influenced by a variety of factors. In fact, it is fairly easy to create contexts where people choose certain options. Many of these tendencies are called "framing effects," because the perceived context or way the choices are "framed" make a big difference, even for situations that are otherwise equivalent. Framing effects have been noted for centuries, and many were summarized by Kahneman and Tversky (1982).

To understand some of these framing effects, we need to distinguish between two types of decision making choices: risky and riskless. A risky choice is one where there is a probability or chance of different possibilities occurring. For example, if you decide to spend money on a lottery, there is an unknown outcome. You may win a lot of money, or you may not. The final outcome is not made by your decision; your decision simply enters you into a probabilistic situation. A riskless choice is one where the ultimate outcome is decided by the choice. For example, if you decide to invest your money in a bank account and earn interest, you have made a riskless choice.

Different people are comfortable with different amounts of risk. Some people tend to be risk-seeking and look for situations where the ultimate outcome is unknown. Other people tend to be risk-avoiding and look for the "sure bets." Regardless of your comfort level with risk, your tendency to be risk-avoiding or risk-seeking can be influenced by the context within which the options are presented to you. A common finding in the experimental literature on decision making is that people tend to be risk-seeking when the options available to them seem to involve losses. People tend to be risk-avoiding when the options available to them seem to involve gains. Interestingly, as long as you are honest in your responses, this effect does not disappear even when you know of its influence on you.

This demonstration shows how the framing of the options to look as gains or losses changes your willingness to deal with risk. Decision making experiments tend to be done by asking participants to imagine themselves in a particular situation and then to choose between two or more possibilities. This approach depends on the honesty of the participants. You can easily get invalid results by refusing to answer honestly.

This demonstration also shows another common finding in studies of decision making: changes tend to be more important than final states. All of the questions in the experiment involve sums of money (U.S. dollars). There are pairs of questions that are equivalent in the sense that you will reach the same absolute amount of money, or possible amount of money in a risky option, for either question in a pair. If your decision making was based solely on the final amount of money you would have, you would make the same decision for either member of the pair. Odds are, however, that you will behave quite differently across the pair members; choosing the risky option for one question but the riskless option for the other. Many aspects of economics and business pertain to properties of decision making. The old business adage of focusing on the "bottom line" is an effort to avoid the tendency among people to focus on changes instead of absolute effects. Characteristics of decision-making tendencies are also well known by advertisers and politicians, who will sometimes influence people's decisions by framing options in a certain way. You can also learn to make better decisions (in the sense of making decisions that are more in line with your beliefs) by taking a more objective approach in your daily life, and by learning some details about statistical reasoning.

After clicking on the start button, a window will appear. Start a trial by clicking on the Next trial button. You will be asked to imagine that you have (above and beyond what you currently own) an extra amount of money. This amount will vary across questions. You will see two options and you will be asked which one you would prefer. For example, you might see:

Imagine you have just received your paycheck worth $350

Which would you choose?

A: A sure loss of $60

OR

B: 0.4 probability of losing $0
and 0.6 probability of losing $100

If you pick Option A, you will have a final total of $290 because you are guaranteed to lose $60. If you pick Option B, you might lose nothing (and keep all $350) but you might lose $100 and end up with only $250. For this example, if you picked Option B you would lose $100 six times out of ten.

To indicate your preference, type the letter that corresponds to the option that you think is best. If you prefer Option A, press the A button. If you prefer Option B, press the B button. In making your decision, try to imagine what the money would actually be worth to you. For example, if you owe a threatening loan shark $290, perhaps it is better to pick the riskless situation (option A) so that you are certain to be able to completely pay off the debt. On the other hand, if you really need $350, and having $290 will not suffice, perhaps it is better to take the risky option (option B) and hope you keep all the money. You should make the decision relative to your real world situation (which is hopefully not so stressful). Some people will like option A best and some will like option B best; there are no absolutely correct answers.

Other trials include options with gains instead of losses of money. The starting amount of money, the loss or gain amounts, and the probabilities vary across trials. After you are satisfied with your choice, press the space bar to start the next trial. There are a total of 30 trials.

When the experiment finishes, a new window will appear that reports the percentage of times you selected the risky option (option B), for the gain questions and the loss questions. The expected result is that the percentage will be higher for the questions where the options available are both losses of money than for the questions where the options available are both gains of money.

Additional References

Frisch, D. (1993). Reasons for framing effects. *Organizational Behavior and Human Decision Processes, 54,* 399-429.

Johnson, R. D. (1987). Making decisions when information is missing: Inferences, biases, and framing effects. *Acta Psychologica, 66,* 69-72.

Kahneman, D. & Tversky, A. (1984). Choices, values, and frames. *American Psychologist, 39,* 341-350.

Basic Questions

1. Do your results confirm the framing effect? Explain your answer.

2. Give an example (not presented here) of a risky decision and a riskless decision.

3. From your experience with this demonstration, suggest a way that might reduce the framing effect.

Advanced Questions

A. From the group mean percentage of times that the risky option B was chosen for the loss questions and for the gain question, decide if the framing effect was confirmed.

Discussion Questions

1. Suggest some reasons why the framing effect occurs.

Judgment – Typical Reasoning

Tversky and Kahneman (1983) are well known for their research showing that people's estimates of probability are often very different from the objective probabilities. The reason, they argue, is that people often use heuristics to help them estimate the answer. Heuristics can be seen as sacrificing some accuracy for an increase in speed. By using heuristics, people can come up with an answer very quickly that is usually good enough for day to day purposes. These heuristics, however, can lead to incorrect judgments.

One of the most striking errors is known as the conjunction fallacy. In its most simple form, it says that people think that having both A and B occur is more likely than having just A occur or just B occur. According to objective probabilities, the probability of two events occurring has to be less than the probabilities of either of the events happening by themselves. In some circumstances, however, people are more likely to say the conjunction (having both events occur) is more likely.

In particular, the conjunction fallacy is more likely when the items are typical than atypical. For example, read the following:

> Julie is 26 years old, has a degree in physical education, has been physically fit since childhood, and loves the outdoors.

People think it is more likely that Julie is a ski instructor who also teaches aerobics (a conjunction involving an activity thought to more typical of ski instructors) than that Julie is a librarian who also teaches aerobics (a conjunction involving an activity thought to be less typical of librarians). When the activity is particularly typical, then the conjunction can be thought more likely than the single events (e.g., that Julie is a ski instructor).

This demonstration is based on an experiment by Shafir, Smith, and Osherson (1990). You will read short descriptions about several people, and you will be asked to rate the probability that these people have certain professions and/or engage in certain activities.

After clicking on the start button, a window will appear. Start a trial by clicking once on the "Next Trial" button. You will be shown a short description of a person. Read the description carefully. After each description, you will be asked to judge how likely it is, on a scale from 0 to 7, that the person has a particular profession or engages in a particular activity. For example, you might be asked the following:

> How likely is it that Bob bets on horse racing?

If you are absolutely certain, based on the description of him that you have just read, that Bob would never bet on horse racing, click on the "0 = Impossible" button. If you are absolutely certain that Bob bets on horse racing, click on the "7 = Certain" button.

There are no correct or incorrect answers. Please respond based on the assumption that the person described is a real person. There are only 12 trials, so please read each description carefully before responding.

When the experiment finishes, a new window will appear that reports your mean ratings for each of four types of judgments. There are four types of statements associated with each person's description, but you saw only one. The four statements include one with an event that is not typical given the person's description; one with an event that is very typical; one statement with the atypical event combined with a profession; and one statement with the typical event combined with a profession.

You should find that for the single events, you gave higher ratings for the typical event than for the atypical event. For the conjunctions, you should find that you gave higher ratings for the typical than for the atypical conjunction. You should also find that you have rated conjunctions with typical activities as more likely than single typical events. If you were relying on objective probabilities, the conjunctions should have been rated as less likely than the single events.

Additional References

Fisk, J. & Pidgeon, N. (1997). The conjunction fallacy: The case for the existence of competing heuristic strategies. *British Journal of Psychology*, *88*, p. 1-27.

Fantino, E., Kulik, J., Stolarz-Fantino, S., & Wright, W. (1997). The conjunction fallacy: A test of averaging hypotheses. *Psychonomic Bulletin & Review*, *4*, p. 96-101.

Basic Questions

1. Bob is 32 and is very athletic. When he is not playing sports, he has his head buried in a book about health and fitness.
   - Give an example of each of the four scenarios used in this lab (single typical, single atypical, conjunctive atypical, conjunctive atypical)?

2. Why would your chances of finding a good used car decrease if your requirements are that it has to be red, a 4-door, good on gas and under $1000?

3. You are writing a paper on gambling for Health Psychology. You are frustrated because the Internet search is not helping you to find any scientific journals on the effects of gambling on your immune system, but you know they exist. You are using some the keywords, "gambling" and "health" and "immune system". How could you change your search strategy so you could increase the number of hits you get?

4. Your duties as summer recreation director for a sport's camp is to find quality camp counselors. You are really busy with final exams and don't have a great deal of time to interview a lot of people. How could you reduce the number of applications that you receive without cutting the quality of the applicants?

5. Saturday afternoon you go to the local library to do some research for a paper. You are having trouble finding a journal so you look for the librarian. You notice 2 people who look like they are working, one is a female about 45 and is wearing glasses and the other is a female about 25 without glasses. You immediately approach the older female who refers you to the other woman as the librarian. Why did you quickly assume the older woman was the librarian?

Advanced Questions

A. Police profilers are portrayed on television as being able to determine, with accuracy, the probability that an individual has committed a crime based on a combination of personality traits and situational circumstances. Why does this seem like an inaccurate way of determining guilt given what you have learned from this lab?

B. Some people with specific occupations rely on making life and death decisions quickly. When accuracy is more important than speed, what type of reasoning should individuals adopt and why? (Think of the 4 scenarios discussed in this lab.)

C. You are a doorman in a popular nightclub. Lately there have been a number of fights in the club and your boss wants you to stop them before they start. While scanning the crowd for potential fights, 2 large groups of individuals come in. You can't watch both groups simultaneously, so you have to decide which group to focus more attention on. One group is made up of longhaired males, while the other group is also made up of some longhaired males and some men with shaved heads with noticeable tattoos. Which group do you think is more likely to start a fight and why? Have you made any errors calculating probability?

Discussion Questions

1. Results from this lab help demonstrate that sometimes we perceive something to be more probable than it really is, resulting in estimation errors. How does this help to explain phobias that people may develop, like fear of flying or the fear of the number 13 (Triskadekaphobia)?

2. What would you suggest a University could do to reduce the number of errors made from stereotyping people or groups of people based on characteristics they portray?

Judgment – Wason Selection Task

Research has shown that people find it very difficult to decide what information is necessary in order to test the truth of an abstract logical reasoning problem. The Wason Selection Task is often used to examine this issue.

A typical experiment using the Wason Selection Task will present some rule, and ask subjects to see if the rule is being violated. Consider the rule: If a card has a D on one side, it has a 3 on the other side. Subjects are aware that on the particular set of cards, each one has a letter on one side and a number on the other side. Four cards are shown, such as those below:

D	K	3	7

Very few people can correctly pick the two cards to turn over to verify the rule. The correct cards are D and 7; most likely, you picked D and 3. Seeing what is on the reverse of the 7 card can lead to falsifying the rule if a D shows up. Seeing what is on the reverse of the 3 card cannot falsify the rule. It can confirm the rule, but not falsify it.

Consider another rule: If you borrow my car, you must fill up the gas tank. Four cards are shown below:

Borrowed Car	Did Not Borrow Car	Empty Gas Tank	Full Gas Tank

Which cards do you turn over to see if the rule is being followed? You should find that now the answer is more obvious: You want to know what's on the reverse of "borrowed car" and "empty gas tank".

This lab is based on a series of experiments reported by Wason & Shapiro (1971). You will be given a series of rules to verify. Half of them are abstract and half are thematic (the same kind of rule shown above about borrowing a car). The basic idea is that you can test rules when you have some knowledge or experience that is appropriate, but not when you lack this experience. In the thematic case, then, you are not really using logic per se but rather your experience. In the abstract case, you cannot use your experience and have to rely solely on logic.

Start a trial by clicking on the Next Trial button. You will see a rule and four buttons. The rule will ask about two kinds of events. Your task is to select two cards to see what is on the other side so that you can see if the rule is true or false. To select a card, simply click on the appropriate button. Once you have clicked on a card, you cannot change your response.

There are 6 trials, 3 with abstract and 3 with thematic rules.

When the experiment finishes, a new window will appear that gives the proportion of correct solutions for both the abstract and the thematic rules. You should find that you did very well on the thematic rules, but quite poorly on the abstract rules. In the thematic case, your knowledge helps you arrive at a correct solution, whereas you have no knowledge to help in the thematic case.

Basic Questions

1. When the conditional rule is stated this way, "if p, then q", this is a(n) _____ (abstract or concrete) statement, whereas "if you get bit by a poisonous snake, you will die is an example of a(n) _____ statement.

2. Of the two types of conditional rules, abstract or concrete, which is usually easier for people to solve?

3. You tell your brother in the morning after he eats his breakfast, "If you leave the milk out of the refrigerator, it will go bad", could you assume that your brother left the milk out if you tasted the milk that evening and it was bad? Why or why not.

4. Your biggest pet peeve is liars; you can't stand it when people lie to you. You think your friend lied to you but you are not sure. You tell him that if you catch him lying to you, you will never speak to him again. Your friend wants to test your rule, so he lies to you, but you do not stop speaking to him. Can your friend say that your rule was not correct? If he stopped speaking to you a week later, what would have to be true to make this a logically correct rule?

Advanced Questions

A. You are a division manager for a large corporation that makes toothpicks. You have noticed that your division is spending a lot in wages, but your toothpick productivity is decreasing. You want to fire those individuals who are on the payroll, but are not packaging at least 100 boxes of toothpicks per day. Give an example of the conditional rule you could send out to the members of your division so that is they broke it, they would be fired immediately.

B. Your mother made a couple of batches of cookies and they are in the kitchen cooling. As she is leaving the kitchen she tells that you can have some cookies, but tells you can't eat the batch of cookies on the green plate because she mixed up the ingredients and put rat poison in them and you will get sick if you eat them. She says it is safe to eat the cookies on the yellow plate. Your get distracted by the phone before you get to the cookies. When you get off the phone, you look at the plates while trying to remember which plate of cookies to eat from. If you had to put this example on cards (like in the lab), what would the four conditions be? Which conditional rule would you not want to test?

C. You are doing some volunteer work in the hospital one summer when you run into a big problem. The nurse on duty tells you that if you do not give Mr. Jones his medication at 4:00 pm, he will not be very cooperative for the night nurse. The following day, you read the note from the night nurse who is not happy with you because Mr. Jones was not very cooperative. What are the two possible assumptions that the night nurse could have about Mr. Jones' medication on the previous day? Which assumption would make this rule logically correct? Which assumption is logically incorrect to make?

Discussion Questions

1. Discuss some further examples of conditional rules that society places on us every day so we can function properly as a group, instead of as selfish individuals. These can be legal, moral, psychological, etc. rules

2. Discuss why some researchers feel the Wason Selection task may be related to memory processes and not deductive reasoning? Did you find that you were remembering a rule that helped you with the examples in the lab or were you analyzing the logic of the rules?

GLOSSARY

ABSOLUTE IDENTIFICATION helps to explain why it is difficult to identify objects when they differ from other objects to be identified by only one dimension (for example length). Identification improves if the items vary by more than one dimension.

ATTENTION The ability to selectively choose some stimuli for processing and ignore others

ATTENTIONAL BLINK the brief time after paying attention to a stimulus during which attention cannot be focused on a subsequent stimulus

APPARENT MOTION The perceived motion of a single light that results when stationary lights are flashed on and off in rapid succession.

AUTOMATIZED BEHAVIOR A behavior that proceeds without direct interaction once the series of movements is initiated

BLIND SPOT The functionally blind area in each eye located at the optic disk

CATEGORICAL PERCEPTION-DISCRIMINATION refers to the ability to detect whether 2 stimuli are the same or different.

CATEGORICAL PERCEPTION-IDENTIFICATION refers to the point at which one's categorical perception changes from identifying one distinct item from another.

CLASSICAL CONDITIONING is a type of learning in which a stimulus acquires the capacity to stimulate a response that was originally brought about by another stimulus. Learning by association.

CONJUNCTIVE SEARCH The type of search performed in a visual search task when the target requires the presence of one attribute and another attribute together

CORRECT REJECTION A trial in a signal detection experiment in which a participant correctly reports that a target was not present

C A measure of response bias in a signal detection experiment; a value greater than zero indicates a conservative bias and a value less than zero indicates a liberal bias

DISTRACTOR TASK A task (such as mental arithmetic) designed to prevent active rehearsal of information in short term memory

D-prime (d') A measure of participant sensitivity in a signal detection experiment; the larger d' the greater the sensitivity

ENCODING SPECIFICITY the memory of an event is related to the interaction between the properties of the encoded event and the properties of the encoded retrieval information.

EXHAUSTIVE SEARCH A search of memory that ends only after all items have been accessed

EXPLICIT LEARNING is when one consciously or intentionally acquires knowledge about a stimulus or a task

FALSE ALARM A trial in a signal detection experiment in which a participant incorrectly reports a target when it was not present

FORGOT IT ALL ALONG is a memory phenomenon where an individual experiences an event, then fails to remember that event for a period of time but then later recalls that event.

FOVEA The central area on the retina of each eye that is densely packed with light sensitive receptors; we turn our foveas toward whatever we are looking at

FRAMING EFFECTS The influence of context on the way people make decisions

GESTALT PSYCHOLOGY is an area of psychology that follows the premise that people organize their perceptions according to certain patterns, so that what you see as a whole is not equal to the sum of its parts.

HEURISTICS are quickly produced problem solving "short cuts" that may not always lead to a correct answer.

HIT A trial in a signal detection experiment in which a participant correctly identifies a target

ICONIC STORE A visual sensory storage system lasting a few hundred milliseconds

IMPLICIT LEARNING is when one unconsciously or unintentionally acquires knowledge about a stimulus or a task.

INTERSTIMULUS INTERVAL (ISI) The period of time between the offset of a first stimulus and the onset of a second stimulus.

IRRELEVANT SPEECH EFFECT the memory for a list of items may be impaired when an irrelevant speech (auditory) stimulus follows the presentation of the list, even when the list is visually presented.

KORTE'S LAWS Statements describing aspects of apparent motion, such as the relation between the ISI and the spatial separation required for motion to be perceived.

LEXICON A metal dictionary containing information about a word's meaning, its part of language, and its relationship to other words

Log(alpha) A measure of participant sensitivity in a signal detection experiment

MASKING The impaired performance on judgement of a target stimulus due to the presentation of another stimulus (the mask)

MEMORY SPAN The capacity of short term or working memory; measured in how many list items a participant can recall in correct order

METACONSTRAST MASKING A special case of masking in which the target and mask have no overlapping contours and the mask is presented after the target

METHOD OF CONSTANT STIMULI A psychophysical method that requires the observer to make judgements about stimuli in terms of whether they are perceived to be greater or less than a standard stimulus

MISS A trial in a signal detection experiment in which a participant fails to detect a target

MODALITY EFFECTS can help to explain why the memory for the last items in a list of items improves when presented in certain modalities, for example when a list is read out loud or is silently mouthed.

MONTY HALL is a classic problem of understanding probability. You are given 3 choices to pick from. When that choice is made, you are asked if you wish to stay with that choice or pick one of the 2 remaining choices. According to the Monty Hall logic, you increase your probability of winning over the long term, if you always switch. Probability increases from 1/3 (0.33) to ½ (0.50).

MULLER-LYER ILLUSION The "arrow" illusion in which the shank with the outward wings appears longer than the shank with the inward wings even tough the shanks are the same objective length

OPERATION SPAN refers to the number of sequential operation-word strings that a participant can attend to. The greater your operation span, the greater the attention span.

OPTIC DISK The region in each eye where the optic nerve exits; it contains no light sensitive receptors and produces the blind spot

PARALLEL SEARCH A search of memory in which every item is accessed simultaneously

PERCEPTUAL SPAN The amount of information that can be gathered in a single precept

POSITION ERROR GRADIENTS helps to explain the systematic errors that an individual may make when recalling a list of items. Generally adjacent items are mixed up.

PRIMACY EFFECT The first few items in a list are remembered particularly well in a free recall task

PROTOTYPE A mental construct having the critical properties of a concept; used to identify new objects

PSYCHOMETRIC FUNCTION A graph that relates the probability of a certain response to variations in a physical characteristic of a stimulus

PSYCHOPHYSICS A sub discipline of psychology that attempts to relate reported characteristics of perception to physical properties of stimuli that give rise to those reports.

RECENCY EFFECT The last few items in a list are remembered particularly well in a free recall task

RECEPTIVE FIELD Any stimulus that changes a neuron's firing rate

REMEMBER/KNOW is a recognition memory phenomenon that ties to distinguish between memories that one *remembers*, consciously aware of some aspect of the original learning situation or *knows*, they have no conscious awareness of the learning situation.

SELF REFERENT EXAMPLES these are examples that are personally relevant. These examples tend to improve one's memory.

SELF-TERMINATING SEARCH A search of memory that ends as soon as a match has been found

SERIAL SEARCH A search of memory in which items are accessed successively

SIGNAL DETECTION A procedure that provides a separate measure of sensitivity and response bias for situations in which observers are required to detect the presence of a faint target

SIGNAL DETECTION THEORY proposes that the detection of a stimulus involves sensory processes as well as decision processes, which are both related to stimulus intensity.

SIMON EFFECT response time may be reduced and accuracy may increase when a stimulus is presented in the same relative location as the response required.

SPATIAL CUEING participant responses may be faster at locating a target that is previously cued but slower when the target's location is not previously cued.

STROOP EFFECT The difficulty participants have in naming ink colors of color words when the ink colors and the color words do not agree

SUFFIX EFFECT the recall of the last item in a list that is read aloud may be impaired if the list is followed by an irrelevant suffix

TYPICAL REASONING when estimating likelihoods, individuals tend to make reasoning errors based on time saving heuristics and generalizations. One reasoning error we make is the *conjunction fallacy*, where 2 typical events seem more probable that one typical event.

VISUAL SCOTOMA Damaged part of the retina causing a blind spot

VISUAL SEARCH A task in which the participant searches a visual image for the presence of a particular item; the participant responds as quickly as possible once the item is found or once it is certain that the item is not present

VON RESTORFF EFFECT is a recall memory phenomenon that helps to explain why the memory of an item in a list improves if it is distinctive from the surrounding items.

WASON SELECTION TASK this task is used to test the truth of an abstract logical rule. Four cards with information on both sides are displayed and participants are asked which 2 cards must be turned over in order to verify the given rule.

WORD SUPERIORITY EFFECT Letters that are part of words are recognized more easily than letters in isolation

NOTES

NOTES

NOTES